One of the most common mistakes we make as parents is to assume that our children are "just like me." A father who enjoys leadership and taking risks, for example, may be frustrated with a son who is cautious and moves at a slower pace. *Different Children, Different Needs* offers practical help for any parent to truly understand how their children behave and then make adjustments to meet their unique needs. This book will help you look at your children in a totally different way.

Dennis Rainey
Executive Director, FamilyLife

*Different Children, Different Needs* is one of the most comprehensive manuals I've read on parenting. It is easy-to-understand reading which follows a hands-on, do-as-you-read format, enabling the reader to learn new parenting methods and procedures in a step-by-step process. The results are a better understanding of ourselves as parents, as well as our children with their many differences and distinctions. Charlie Boyd ties all of the information to basic how-tos which are practical and enlightening. I believe this book will make a positive difference in families that care enough to apply what it teaches.

Zig Ziglar
Chairman, The Zig Ziglar Corp.

I've had the privilege of knowing Charlie Boyd for years, and watching him develop an outstanding ministry to parents across the country. Now he's taken many of those tested principles and created a powerful tool for building close-knit families—*Different Children, Different Needs.* If you're ready to decrease distance in your home, and to <u>increase</u> closeness, insight, and communication, this book is for you.

John Trent
President, Encouraging Words

# Different Children Different Needs

# Different Children Different Needs

## The Art of Adjustable Parenting

CHARLES F. BOYD
WITH DAVID BOEHI

Sisters, Oregon

DIFFERENT CHILDREN, DIFFERENT NEEDS

published by Multnomah Books
*a part of the Questar publishing family*



*International Standard Book Number:* 0-88070-685-6

Cover design by Bruce DeRoos

Edited by Stephen T. Barclift

Printed in the United States of America



For information:
QUESTAR PUBLISHERS, INC.
POST OFFICE BOX 1720
SISTERS, OREGON 97759

94 95 96 97 98 99 00 01 02 — 10 9 8 7 6 5 4 3 2 1

*To my parents, Frank and Betty Boyd,*
*who let me be myself.*

*To my wife, Karen,*
*who is helping me become more*
*than I could ever be alone.*

*And to my children, Chad, Kristi, and Callie,*
*who I pray will benefit most*
*from the material in this book.*

# CONTENTS

# PREFACE

This is not a book. Oh, I know it looks like a book and feels like a book. But I would like to ask you not to think of it as a book; at least not the way you think of most other books.

Most books are read and then put back on the shelf. They inform and entertain, but after they are read, they are forgotten. Even the advice in "how to" books is often ignored. Used book stores are full of books that people felt were no longer valuable enough to keep.

I hope it will be different with this one. The contents of the following pages can shape your thinking about your job as a parent in ways you may not expect. It's my prayer that when you finish the last page you will not be the same, or at least you won't think in the same way—about your mate, your children, your parents, or anyone else. This material had that kind of impact for me and my wife, Karen, and I've seen it do the same time and again in the lives of those who attend parenting or marriage seminars that present what you are about to read.

Now, this is not the last book on parenting you'll ever have to read. Far from it. There are many things you need to know about parenting that are not mentioned in this book. I've included a resource section in the back to help you as you seek to equip yourself to become a better parent.

But *Different Children, Different Needs* lays a key foundation. Based on the biblical teaching of Proverbs 22:6, the principles in this book can become the backbone for everything you do as a parent. If you don't practice the "big picture" principle that is presented in the following pages, your kids will be negatively affected. But if you take Proverbs 22:6 seriously and you seek to apply what you find in this book, your children will come to understand how God has designed and gifted them. They will grow to have both a sense of confidence and a sense of belonging.

# ACKNOWLEDGMENTS

Many people played key roles in helping and encouraging me to write this book. I especially want to thank the leadership team at Carlson Learning Company who supported me in this effort: Tom Ritchey, Sara Lykken, Barbara Meiss, and Clyde Hanson.

A number of associates and friends have also helped. Rich Meiss made my first publication, *The Couple's Profile*, a reality, and that led to many other open doors. Dan Kaufman, Rosemarie Magee, Charlotte Miller, Brian Briley, and Kay Dalby read early drafts and made many helpful suggestions.

Phone conversations with Sandra Merwin and Robert Rohm, storytellers *par excellence*, were deeply stimulating and informative. Dave Tarpley's lunchtime conversations cheered me on and kept me writing when I wanted to quit.

Steve Farrar first encouraged me to write a book on this topic and then helped me make the key contacts with publishers that eventually led to my signing with Questar. Wes Neal graciously allowed me to adapt his outstanding material on strengths and weaknesses and include it in Appendix A.

The Questar team of Donald Jacobson, Stephen Barclift, Dan Rich, and Michele Tennesen have all been a delight to work with.

Doug Daily introduced me to the DiSC™ model in such a way that it literally changed my life.

In spite of the help and insight from the people listed above, this book wouldn't have made it to press if it weren't for Dave Boehi. Dave came alongside me with skill, creativity, and expertise—honing, distilling, refining, and clarifying my thoughts and ramblings. He worked tirelessly to make the deadline, as his family well knows. I couldn't have done it without him.

I would like to mention that most examples used throughout this book are from my own family experience, but many are from the experience of others who have shared willingly, though they requested that their real names not be used.

---

*Author's note: An attempt has been made to give "equal time" to masculine and feminine pronouns. I've tried to avoid the clumsy "s/he" and "him/her" by using feminine terms in the even numbered chapters and masculine terms in the odd numbered chapters.*

PART I

# "TRAIN UP A CHILD..."

CHAPTER ONE

# PARENT POLLUTION

"Why can't my mother accept me for who I am? Whenever I'm with her, she reminds me that I can't sew like her, I can't cook like her, and I don't keep the house as neat and clean as she does. She criticizes my lifestyle, and accuses me of being vain.

"She has always tried to make me into somebody I'm not. And every time we're together, she constantly picks at me."

How often I have heard those words! How often, too, I have found a distraught child sitting in my office, seeking help on how to deal with a parent who just doesn't understand what makes him special, what makes him unique. What I find most amazing is that these "children" are often in their thirties and forties and still facing a basic problem that was never resolved when they were younger.

This time the words came from Rebecca. Her eyes filled with tears as her anger melted into hurt. She reached for a tissue and broke into deep sobs. Her most recent collision with her mother had occurred just hours before she came to see me.

Rebecca had won an award for her work in a volunteer civic organization and had phoned to tell her mother the good news. As she began describing the awards banquet and the honor she had received, her mother interrupted and said, "I never cared much for those social clubs and that sort of thing. You should spend your time doing something more constructive, rather than flitting around in the limelight. Those kinds of things just give people a big head and they think they are better than everybody else."

Rebecca never had a chance to explain that she had been honored for her volunteer work with children in the inner city. All she heard was criticism. "This was one of the most important days of my life," Rebecca said, "and she could not even say, 'Congratulations,' much less, 'I'm really proud of you.' "

Rebecca had always been an outgoing child who made friends easily and loved being with people. She was naturally enthusiastic about almost any task she put her mind to, and often was able to persuade others to join with her. She was the type who had difficulty hiding her emotions, a fact which she sometimes hated; but that trait only endeared her to her friends and made them feel they could be themselves around her.

Her mother was quite different. She was a quiet, cautious woman who felt uncomfortable in large groups. She enjoyed quiet conversations, sewing, and good books. She kept her house meticulously clean and felt uneasy when everything was not in its place.

As Rebecca grew up, she found herself constantly in trouble for not cleaning the house to her mother's standards. "I can't tell you how many hours I had to work on Saturdays, dusting the furniture over and over until I wiped off every speck of dust. I could never please her."

In her small town, Rebecca always seemed to find her way into the spotlight. Every time she did, her mother scolded her for developing a big head. When Rebecca performed in a school play, her mother warned that she would grow up conceited if she continued seeking applause. When she made the cheer-leading squad, her mother said, "I can't understand why any sensible girl would think *that* is an accomplishment."

Rebecca felt like she was a prisoner to her mother's "shoulds" and "shouldn'ts." Here she was, thirty-five years old, married, mother of two, and still not free. She couldn't enjoy the recognition she had just received because deep in her soul she thirsted for approval from the one woman who seemed unable to give it.

Rebecca was somewhat surprised that her ten-year-old daughter, Laurie, had a great relationship with her grandmother. "Mother and Laurie get along fine. That girl seems content sitting in her room, reading books or playing with her dolls.

*"But I am bound and determined that she will get out and make friends, meet people, and enjoy life."*

Note the irony here? Rebecca couldn't see it, but she was repeating the pattern that had caused her so much anguish. The problem had passed on to one more generation.

## Bending Our Children Out of Shape

Rebecca was struggling with an age-old problem that I call "parent pollution." We all have inherited some. We also will pass some on to our children.

What is parent pollution? Raising your children the way you *think* they ought to go…or want them to go.

That sounds innocent enough, doesn't it? After all, what parent doesn't want the best for his kids? We want them to feel confident, competent, and capable. We want our kids to feel loved, cared for, and valued. We don't set out to intentionally frustrate them or warp them.

Too often, however, we assume that what is "best" means that our children should live their lives according to the script that has worked for us. Without realizing it, we try to create carbon copies of ourselves.

A related problem is seen in the parent who doesn't like certain aspects of his personality or behavior. He doesn't want his children to experience the same failures he has, so if he notices that his children behave like he does, he tries to stamp out the behavior.

In either case, we actually bend our children out of the shape that God has instilled in them. Many problems of low self-esteem and low confidence stem from parents who failed to accept their children for who God had made them to be.

An often-quoted Proverb lays a foundation stone for effective parenting:

> Train a child in the way he should go, and when he is old he will not turn from it.
>
> —Proverbs 22:6

Many Christians assume this verse simply instructs us to take our children to church and keep them in school, off drugs, and out of trouble. Then, even if they stray temporarily from the straight and narrow, when they are old, they will return to the morals and lifestyle they were raised to maintain.

My problem with this popular interpretation is that every child has the capacity to make his own choices. It doesn't take into account the individual will of the child. I've seen too many children who were raised in good Christian homes run wild anyway. Some have never returned to God or their spiritual roots.

The correct interpretation of Proverbs 22:6 has a radically different meaning. The phrase "in the way he should go" does not refer to some prescribed path that every person should follow. In the Hebrew language, the phrase is better rendered, "according to his way." And the Hebrew word for "way" is *derek*, which literally means bent and refers to a unique inner design or direction.

Therefore, a more accurate rendering of this verse would be:

> Adapt the training of your child
> so that it is in keeping with his natural design;
> when he comes to maturity,
> he will not depart from that pattern of life.

This verse actually instructs us to nurture our children according to their nature.

## A Metal That Remembers

Recently I watched an episode of "Beyond 2000" on television's Discovery Channel, and I learned about a new type of metal. This "shape memory alloy," as it was called, could be programmed to "remember" a certain shape. If that original shape was distorted in some way (by twisting and bending it with your hands, for example), it could easily be restored by simply passing it through hot water. Imagine car bodies made of a metal like that—if you had a fender bender, you would simply take your automobile to a nearby car wash and it would be good as new!

As parents, we need to discover our children's natural styles and help each one grow up according to his unique, in-born, God-given design. As they experience the collisions of life, they will be more prone to return to who they really are, rather than becoming permanently bent out of shape. Their self-esteem will remain intact.

Training a child according to his bent is not as easy as it sounds. We usually feel most comfortable with people who are like us. Think of your friendships. Chances are that you know people with many types of personalities, but there's a certain type of person you enjoy most. We tend to like people who are like us.

Many companies I've observed tend to reflect the personalities of their directors. If he is decisive and aggressive, his natural tendency often is to view those qualities as essential for leadership. He may view employees who are more cautious or people-oriented as slow and ineffective.

Over time, you begin to notice that the people in top positions at a company seem to have the same behavioral style—just like the director's. Sometimes this works, but often it does not because the leader fails to recognize that different situations require different styles of leadership.

It's the same with children. God gives many parents children whose bents seems to consistently bend them out of shape! When their children's unique tendencies rub the parents the wrong way, they try to make those differences disappear and replace them with qualities they value. Often, they try to remake their children into their own images.

If you want to have a meaningful relationship with your children, you must understand who they are as God designed them. You must lay aside what *you* want your children to become and spend time getting to know who they *already are.*

Don't misunderstand me. I'm not suggesting you let your children be in charge and set their own course. They need your supervision and guidance. They need to learn how to live, and how not to live. They need you to help them develop convictions and character.

As you pursue these goals, however, it's important for you to understand how to adapt your parenting to meet the individual needs of your children. On one hand, your job is to bend and shape your children as they grow up. But on the other, your job is to provide the home environment and encouragement that will allow their *natural* bents to develop.

### PARABLE OF THE PLANTS

Imagine you have two children. View them as two different seeds that God has placed in your hand. He doesn't tell you what kind of plant those seeds will grow to become; He simply tells you to cultivate them so they will grow up healthy and fruitful.

You know there are certain things every plant needs: water, sunlight, rich soil, carbon dioxide. You provide the basics, and before long those seeds begin to sprout. Soon you have two green, growing young plants.

With each passing week, they begin to look different. Soon they flower and begin to produce the first buds of fruit. It is then you realize that you have been given an apple tree and an orange tree.

Now you must begin cultivating those trees differently. They require different amounts of water and fertilizer, you prune them differently, you must care for them differently. All this makes perfect sense because an apple tree is different from an orange tree.

This is a parable of parenting. When God gives you children, He very often gives you apples and oranges—and perhaps some pears and peaches as well. You give your kids the same basics: things like love, affirmation, meaningful touch, a feeling of belonging and significance. But as they grow older, you begin to notice what makes each child unique and special—and you adjust your style of parenting to cultivate each child according to his natural tendencies.

Understanding each child's personal style is only half the challenge in overcoming parent pollution. You also must learn how God has designed you.

Knowing who you are and how you feel about yourself plays an important part in how you interact with your children. You need to become aware of how your style may complement or clash with your children's styles.

In the following chapters we will look at "the art of adjustable parenting," or parenting by design, an approach to raising your kids that takes into account both how God has designed you and how He has designed your children. I'll show you a simple, practical model that will enable you to:

- Understand your natural bent and the way it affects your parenting style.
- Discover your children's design.
- Compare your style and needs to those of your children.
- Adjust your parenting style to better meet your children's needs.

- Enhance communication between you and your children.
- Reduce common areas of conflict.
- Create an atmosphere of encouragement and cooperation in your home.

The bottom line is this: Parenting by design is a method you can use to adjust your parenting to meet the needs of each of your children—and you don't have to have a degree in psychology to understand it.

This book will permanently change the way you look at your kids. It will give you a language that describes and honors the differences you observe in your children. You will learn skills that help you interact with different children in different ways, according to their individual bents.

As a result, your kids will feel highly valued. They will feel that you understand, accept, and respect them for who they are and not for who you want them to be. That can allow them to grow up with healthy self-respect and a greater tolerance for different types of people who come into their lives.

What you read in this book will not give you the answer to every parenting problem. There are many other parenting principles that you need to learn and apply. In Appendix C, I've included a list of recommended parenting books that address many of those principles.

But I believe Proverbs 22:6 is the starting point. If you do not know your child, you cannot understand your child. If you do not understand your child, you cannot communicate love to your child.

You've probably met many adults like Rebecca. Perhaps her story echoes your experience with your own parents. The good news is that you can stop the flow of parent pollution by accepting your children for who they are. And in doing so, you set them free to become the men and women God intended them to be.

CHAPTER TWO

# THE EPITAPH OF THE UNACCEPTED

As a pastor, one crucial responsibility I've assumed is that of "breakfast chaplain" at a local McDonald's™. Through the years I've come to know many of the regular morning patrons, and because I always seem to be laboring on some project, they frequently ask me, "What are you working on today?"

One of these friends is Amy, a local high school English teacher. Recently, when I told her about my latest project—this book—she sat up and said, "I have something you have to read!" At our next meeting, she handed me a stack of papers her students had written. Few things have sobered me more dramatically than what I read that day. Parent pollution starts early and has devastating affects on our children.

Amy had given two assignments to her class. The first was to write a "solution" poem. Several of the students wrote of trying to please their parents. Here's one example:

***Pleasing My Parents***

I would love to make mom and dad happy.
I try and try,
I always fail.
I work too slow
and I don't do enough.
I ask for help to understand.
What do I do?
Sometimes, I just feel like giving up.
I know I must communicate,
Even though it sounds simple.
It is a boundary that consists of a steel wall.
I will conquer it.

Even more painful were some of the papers from the second assignment: "Write your own epitaph." As I read through the papers, I caught a glimpse of the despair some kids feel as they seek to understand where they stand in the world. One girl, whom Amy described as "very cheerful, almost angelic," evidently had much more churning inside of her than appeared on the surface:

There once was a girl,
Her name was Sarah.
From the outside, she seemed perfect,
But on the inside, she was really messed up.
Because Sarah was the oldest daughter of four,
She had a lot of pressures put on her.
She couldn't handle life anymore,
Her grades were failing and her morals were wrong.
Sarah went out with her so-called "friends,"
She never came home.
Her body was found floating in the river on July 2, 1992.

And then there was the piece titled, "Epitaph of the Unaccepted." It was highly creative, almost surreal in its tone, and yet I could see that here was another child crying out for someone to tell her she was loved and valued, just as she was:

*Epitaph of the Unaccepted*

When I was born, my first inclination was to live.
But the unaccepting substance of society killed my mind.
I knew not why such nominally beneficial rituals grazed my subconscious,
Perhaps my mind was too complicated for them to accept.
These penalties prescribed by tradition,
A tradition of mind hampering this fine commodity of being forever eternal.
It was once said that life is a mingled yarn, so mingled in fact as to choke individuality out of the original.
In closing, a question will be asked,
It's opinion,
Is this life?
Or is this death?

## CULTIVATING THE UNIQUENESS OF EACH CHILD

What makes children feel this way? What makes them conclude that pleasing their parents is as difficult as penetrating a steel wall? No parent would want their son or daughter to write something like these poems. But what are parents doing that causes their children to feel so hopeless?

As a child grows up, she learns more and more about herself—what she likes and dislikes, what she can and can't do well. If her unique identity is nurtured—if she is accepted for the person she is—she can grow up confident and competent, with healthy self-respect. However, if pressure is applied for her to conform to what her parents want her to be, she will grow up feeling inadequate and less sure of herself.

The key is for parents to discover and cultivate the uniqueness of each of their children. For your children to develop, you must value their individuality. This takes us back to our basic parenting premise: *Bring your children up in the way they are to go.* As author Elizabeth O'Conner writes:

> Every child's life gives forth hints and signs of the way he is to go. The parent who knows how to meditate stores these hints and signs away and ponders over them. We are to treasure the intimations of the future that the life of every child gives to us so that, instead of unconsciously putting blocks in his way, we help him to fulfill his destiny. This is not an easy way to follow. Instead of telling our children what they should do and become, we must be humble before their wisdom, believing that in them, and not in us, is the secret they need to discover.[1]

## FEARFULLY AND WONDERFULLY MADE

The Bible includes many encouraging passages describing every person's uniqueness. One of my favorites is Psalm 139:13-16, which describes God's personal touch in making each person special and different:

For you created my inmost being;
 you knit me together in my mother's womb.
I praise you because I am fearfully and wonderfully made;
 your works are wonderful,
 I know that full well.
My frame was not hidden from you
 when I was made in the secret place.
When I was woven together in the depths of the earth,
 your eyes saw my unformed body.
All the days ordained for me
 were written in your book
 before one of them came to be.

The original language for the Old Testament was Hebrew. In that language, the words "knit together" and "woven together" are terms which refer to the complex patterns and colors of a weaver or embroiderer. These words took on new meaning for me when my wife, Karen, and I recently purchased a small oriental rug for the entryway of our home. As we talked with the store's sales clerk, I was amazed to learn how the rugs are made.

Each rug is mounted on its own loom. Long, thin threads of the same shape, color, and fabric are strung vertically and attached to the loom. Then individual pieces of dyed wool are hand knotted to the vertical strands. Different colors are chosen and precisely placed to yield an intricate design.

A high-quality oriental rug blends approximately five hundred knots in each square inch of carpet, and over three million knots on an 8- by 12-foot rug. Depending on how many weavers work on a rug that size, it may take more than two years to complete.

What really makes the best rugs stand out, the sales clerk said, is how their designs emerge from the mind and personality of the "master weaver." My mind jumped to Psalm 139. Each of us is a unique tapestry, woven together with intricate patterns and colors. Just think: Over six billion people live on our planet, and no two of us are the same.

You and your children were created by God in infinite wisdom and love, and you reflect His image. He Himself did the weaving while you were still in your mother's womb. What a powerful reminder of the great value He sets on us from before we were born. Your design was set and your days were determined by the hand of God, the Master Weaver.

But there's more here. The psalmist also talks about his "frame" or "bones." As I sifted through commentaries and lexicons for insight into the original meaning of this passage, I found one highly respected commentator, Dr. H. C. Leupold, who asserted that the word actually means "strengths." This author translated the word to mean "potentialities" or "capabilities." He wrote: "The Creator knew the capabilities that this human being would carry within it, seeing that He Himself gave it all it has."[2]

Think about that. When God made you, He placed within you natural strengths and abilities. He wove those into the fabric of your inner being. And those capabilities and potentialities are part of your unique design. They were given to you to be used to accomplish things for Him.

### FILLED WITH SKILL AND UNDERSTANDING

Another fascinating passage is Exodus 35, which describes how Moses and the Israelites built the Tabernacle so that the nation could be continually reminded of God's presence. Note all the phrases which reveal how God gave different people the unique skills needed to build the Tabernacle:

> Every skilled woman spun with her hands and brought what she had spun—blue, purple or scarlet yarn or fine linen. And all the women

who were willing and had the skill spun the goat hair.

Then Moses said to the Israelites, "See, the LORD has chosen Bezalel son of Uri, the son of Hur, of the tribe of Judah, and he has filled him with the Spirit of God, with skill, ability and knowledge in all kinds of crafts—to make artistic designs for work in gold, silver and bronze, to cut and set stones, to work in wood and to engage in all kinds of artistic craftsmanship. And he has given both him and Oholiab son of Ahisamach, of the tribe of Dan, the ability to teach others. He has filled them with skill to do all kinds of work as craftsmen, designers, embroiderers in blue, purple and scarlet yarn and fine linen, and weavers—all of them master craftsmen and designers" (verses 25-26, 30-35).

God put *skill* and *understanding* into the hearts of different men and women to perform different tasks. They had a passion for that work.

When God made you, He put in your heart strengths, capabilities, potential skills, passions, drives, and motivations. He designed you with a certain way of being. As a result, you feel fulfilled when you are acting according to your design—and frustrated when you aren't.

By the way, God did the same thing when He designed each of your children.

### YOUR BEHAVIORAL STYLE

To parent by design, you need to understand how God has designed you and your children. One of the primary indications of God's design can be found in your behavior—your way of seeing and doing things. Each person has a unique behavioral style.

Your behavioral style plays a dominant role in how you live because it's *permanent*, it's *consistent*, and it *controls your behavior*. It gives evidence that you are not a haphazard collection of possibilities, but a person endowed with highly detailed gifts and abilities.[3]

*Your style is permanent.* Though your overall personality is influenced by your parents and teachers and the good and bad things that happen to you as you grow up, your inborn behavioral style stays with you. Look at these examples:

- Tommy was a child who acquired merit badges at age ten and became an Eagle scout at seventeen. He graduated from college in mechanical engineering and landed a top-paying job with a major corporation at age twenty-four. By age thirty-seven, he moved to the top in his field.
- At age ten, Charlie enjoyed taking clocks and radios apart to see how they worked. While in college he frequently remained after

class to continue an assignment—such as dissecting a sheep's brain or taking a chemistry experiment one step further. At age forty-two, he now works as a problem-solving consultant for a large pharmaceutical company in the east.

- Katherine grew up liking everything in its place. She would spend hours organizing her closets and rearranging furniture in her bedroom. At age thirty, her friends frequently complimented her on how she managed to keep her home so neat and clean while at the same time juggling a part-time job at a major department store. Now, at fifty-one, she is the hospitality director at a large downtown church.
- Tina was a soft-hearted child who would cry herself to sleep when she saw someone killed on television. While in high school, she worked as a candy striper at a local hospital. She went on to major in social work in college, and now at age twenty-nine, she works with inner-city children and listens empathetically to the people in her counseling practice. She confesses that she still has trouble keeping her emotions in check and is often moved to tears in her sessions.

A common thread runs through these stories. In each case, the individual's behavioral style remained constant, no matter what the age or circumstances.

Of course, as you walk with Christ you will become more spiritually and emotionally mature. God wants your *character* to become more Christlike. However, your God-given behavioral style changes no more than the nature of an oak tree. An oak may have green leaves during one season, orange during another, or no leaves at all, but it is still an oak. At times, you may also appear different, but your fundamental behavioral style remains unchanged.

One more thing: The fact that your style is permanent does not mean you are enslaved to one way of being. I'm simply saying that there is a pattern to who we are, and that pattern is consistent.

How many times have you said about someone, "I just knew he would act that way!" or "Isn't that just like her?" We tend to react to people and circumstances in a characteristic manner.

If you see a traffic light changing from green to yellow, how do you react? Do you have a tendency to "gun it and run it" in an attempt to beat the red light, or do you usually play it conservatively and hit the brakes? Chances are you have a "yellow light" style that is consistent. You may not always do the same thing, but more often than not you do.

Here's another test you can try: Place this book down and cross your arms. Look down at your arms. Did you place your left arm over your right, or vice versa? Now cross your arms the other way. Feels pretty awkward, doesn't it?

In the same way, we consistently use patterns of behavior because they are comfortable to us. They fit us. I'm not saying that we are locked into one way of doing something, but we tend to repeat the same behavior in similar situations.

Your style also influences your behavior. If you like challenges, you will take risks. If you like to inspire others, you look for people to lead. If you are motivated to be a team player, you will look for a partner. If you fear making mistakes, you will take necessary precautions to ensure accuracy.

In their book *Finding a Job You Can Love,* Ralph Mattson and Arthur Miller comment on this same concept. "You and your pattern are one. You seek work and people and the church and theology and politics—and everything else in life of importance to you—through your motivational pattern, which is to say, your way of seeing and acting."[4]

By the way, personality and behavioral style are related, but not the same. Personality consists of everything you are—your inborn temperament plus your life experience. This includes genetic traits, needs, drives, values, intelligence, parental upbringing, educational background, how you respond—wisely or unwisely—to your past experiences, cultural background, ingrained social norms, religious beliefs, likes, dislikes, strengths, and weaknesses. Personality is a complex blending of everything that makes up who you are.

Behavioral style is the *outward expression* of who you are, and it may change from context to context. For example, you may not act exactly the same at work as you do at home. Your parenting style may be different from your work and social style. As Tom Ritchey, president of Carlson Learning Company, puts it, "Behavioral style is not who you are, but what you do with who you are." This distinction is important to understand and will become even more clear as we look more closely in the following chapters at our parenting styles.

## THE POTTER-CLAY MENTALITY

One reason it's so critical to learn what makes you and your children individuals is that it takes a lot of pressure off your shoulders. Take the story of Jim and Shannon. When their son Joseph was still a baby, Jim would daydream about what his son might become. "This little guy could become an Olympic champion...or a professional baseball player."

Shannon was dreaming big, too, but differently: "Maybe he'll be a Nobel Prize winner, or a concert pianist...or even the doctor who finds the cure for cancer!" With the right love and guidance, this amazing child would surely become the star he was meant to be.

As Joseph grew, Jim and Shannon's visions of greatness appeared justified. He was the brightest child in preschool and way ahead of other four-year-olds in his swim class. In kindergarten, his IQ tested at 135. Jim and Shannon enrolled him in piano lessons, chauffeured him to soccer and T-Ball, and bought him piles of books and every kind of educational toy imaginable.

Then something horrible happened. In the third grade, Joseph got a D in math. The teacher told the disheartened parents that Joseph wasn't working up to his potential. He was very bright, but he was also lazy.

Jim and Shannon were frantic. How could their brilliant little boy not want to do his best? No matter how hard they begged, pleaded, or threatened, Joseph refused to work hard. By the time he was eleven, Joseph was easygoing and laid back, had a B–average in school, had dropped out of piano lessons, and was the second worst hitter on his Little League team.

How do you think Shannon and Jim felt? What were they thinking?

Right. They wondered where *they* went wrong.

If you believe that how your children turn out is purely a function of what you do, then you are setting yourself up to feel like a failure.

According to the potter-clay mentality, children are born as a blank slate; parents are responsible for shaping their personalities, their potential, their character. I only agree with this mentality up to a point. Parents play a critical role in molding their children—especially in the area of character and moral values. What many people fail to realize, however, is that God gives each child a unique design that will not change.

Most experts believe that while parents certainly influence the personality of their offspring, children are born with their own innate temperament traits. In a landmark study, Stella Chess and her husband, Alexander Thomas, both medical doctors and professors of psychiatry at New York University, followed 133 children from infancy to adulthood. They found that two main forces were at work in shaping their subjects' personalities: one was a youngster's temperament, and the other was how the parents responded to that temperament. In other words, who children become is a function of both nature and nurture.

Evelyn B. Thoman, Ph.D., a child-development researcher at the University of Connecticut, explains the problem this way:

> Baby boomers, who typically have enormously high expectations for themselves, tend to see every real or imagined imperfection in their child as a sign that they have failed. They keep straining to create their fantasy of the ideal child instead of appreciating the real child they actually have.[5]

Recently I ran across a wall hanging with a bit of folk wisdom upon it: "Children are not things to be molded, but people to be unfolded." Consistent parenting does not mean treating each of your children the same way. Isn't it true that you want your mate, your friends, and your co-workers to take into consideration your likes and dislikes, wants and needs? Your children do as well. Consistent parenting means treating different children differently.

The bottom line is this: If you try to force a child into a mold she doesn't fit, you risk sending the message, "I don't love you for who you are. I love you for how close you come to who I want you to be." This message can cause a child to long for a parent's approval the rest of her life.

## A Love Letter

Recently a friend showed me a letter his daughter had just given him. It's the type of letter I wish more kids could send to their parents—and the type I hope my son and daughters feel they can give me when they're older.

> Dad:
>
> I've decided to sit down and write you a love letter. You are so special to me and I'm afraid to leave things unsaid. I have so much respect for you and your faith. The more time I spend around people claiming to be Christians, the more I realize how truly remarkable you are. I say it again and again, meaning it more each time—you are the only person I know who practices everything you preach without having to grit your teeth and angrily struggle the entire way. You've discovered the secret of the "easy yoke" and I admire you greatly for it.
>
> You are one of my best friends. I feel comfortable with you and enjoy our instant level of communication and shared sense of humor. You're my favorite person to go walking with through the woods, collecting leaves, nuts, and rocks along the way...I enjoy our buddy time—I treasure it in my heart.
>
> You are one of the few who accept me as I am—not trying to turn me into an ideal or a carbon copy of themselves. I appreciate that! It's a true love who accepts the whole instead of just the happy.

The very fact that this girl sent her dad such a lovely letter shows me that she feels accepted and secure. Her father did it right.

## NOTES

1. Elizabeth O'Conner, *Eighth Day of Creation* (Waco, Tex.: Word Books, 1971), 18.

2. H.C. Leupold, *Exposition of the Psalms* (Grand Rapids: Baker Book House, 1969), 947.

3. Ralph Mattson and Arthur Miller, *Finding a Job You Can Love* (Nashville: Thomas Nelson, 1982), 60.

4. Ibid., 80.

5. Evelyn B. Thoman, "How to Raise Normal Kids," *New Woman* (December 1991): 53.

# PART II

# UNDERSTANDING

CHAPTER THREE

# WHY YOU ARE WHO YOU ARE

I will never forget the first time I took my son, Chad, on a fishing trip. For weeks I planned for this special day. It would be my first opportunity to initiate my son into a hallowed male-bonding experience. We would rise early, eat a hearty breakfast, and head out to a lake. As the dawn broke, we would slide into the boat and glide across the water, watching the mist rise from the surface.

I would teach Chad the sacred rites of putting on a plastic worm, casting, and working the worm so it would lure the big ones. We would catch our limit of bass. Chad would fall in love with fishing and would beg me to take him again.

Well, reality has a way of making dreams crash to the ground. In the first hour of our "bonding time," Chad managed to:

step off the bank into the mud...
get his line hung up on the first cast...
knock the tackle box over...
cast his line into a tree...
spill his drink into the worm box...
and set a hook in my thumb.

I was, well, just a *little* angry. What happened to my perfect day? This wasn't fishing, it was a joke!

Then I received what I've come to know as the "divine whack on the head." I realized I was so focused on completing the task that I had forgotten the reason for the outing—to spend time with my son. "Maybe fishing isn't the task," I sensed the Lord telling me. "Maybe your son is the task."

## THE FIRST STEP OF PARENTING BY DESIGN

While God had a lesson for me that day about my priorities, what did not change was my basic orientation. I'm the type of guy who thrives on performing tasks and completing projects. I like to stick to business. If we're going to fish, let's fish. If we're going to start a new ministry at church, let's get it up and going, pass it off to someone else, and move on. If we're going to mow the lawn, let's do it and get it over with. Let's not stretch it out by talking to neighbors—let's get the job done.

When I took Chad fishing, the task was simple: catch fish. Every time something happened to block that goal or divert us from the chosen task, I felt more tension and frustration.

My point is that it's good for me to understand who I am and how I behave. Although who I am is as unique as my thumbprint, many of my behaviors are consistent and predictable. That affects everything I do, including my parenting. So *the first step of parenting by design is to understand the behavioral styles of both you and your child.*

In the preceding chapter, I introduced the concept of "behavioral styles." You and your children each display consistent patterns of behavior—different ways of seeing and doing things. So how can you learn what your styles are?

You'll recall that I pictured our internal makeup as being like an oriental tapestry with both vertical and horizontal threads of wool knotted together. The outward expression of who we are—our behavioral style—is likewise based on two major threads: *pace* and *priority.*

Our first step in understanding behavioral style then, is to look at each of these strands. As we will see, when woven together, these two strands produce four definite designs or patterns.

## FAST-PACED, SLOW-PACED

The first strand, a vertical one, I call *pace.* By pace I mean the speed at which a person moves through life. Each of us runs according to an internal motor: some of those motors are running at high speed, while others operate at a slower tempo. One pace is not better than another, they are simply different.

Fast-paced people are characterized by the word "GO," and they stay on the move. They are assertive, and they create a powerful first impression. They are extroverts in the sense that they focus their actions on their outside environment, whether it be people or circumstances.

They are energetic and do almost everything in a hurry. It's no surprise that they easily become impatient with those on the opposite end of the spectrum—those who are slower-paced.

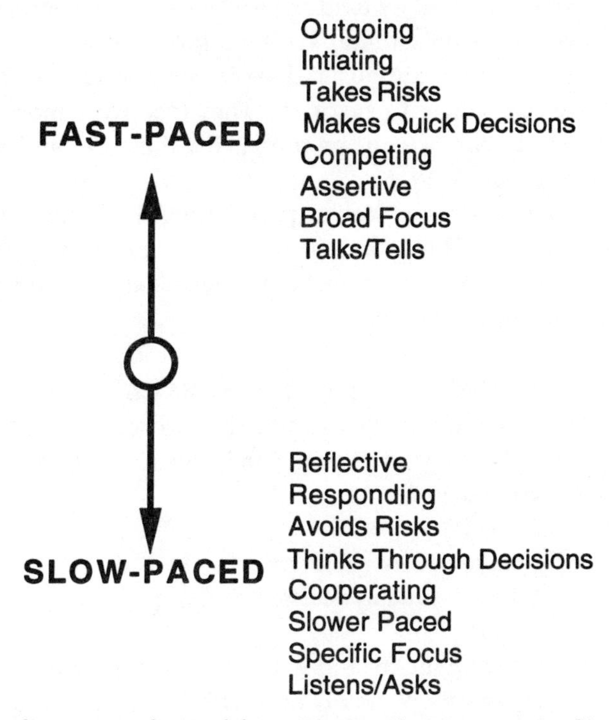


(The above diagram is derived from *The Family Discovery Profile Manual*.[1])

They take social initiative. They get involved in all kinds of organizations, clubs, projects, charities, P.T.A. groups, and church committees. Often they hold leadership positions. They like being in charge of things, not because they like work, but because they are conscious of their personal significance, and like to tell other people what to do. And they can frequently overcommit themselves because they like to juggle several balls at once.

They tend to make quick decisions and like taking risks. They are confident people who readily express their opinions and make emphatic statements. They want action and enjoy competition. I have two books in my study that were no doubt written by fast-paced people: One is entitled, *When I Relax, I Feel Guilty*. The other is *Lead, Follow, or Get Out of the Way*.

Slow-paced people, on the other hand, are characterized by the phrase, "Take your time...not so fast!" Their motto is: "If a job's worth doing, it's worth doing well." They tend to be more quiet, shy, reserved, and self-contained.

As children or adults, they tend to be more security conscious. They move at a slower, more measured pace; therefore, they are slower to make decisions. They are cautious and avoid risky situations. They do not like unplanned changes or surprises. They tend to be more introverted, in that their actions focus on preserving the order and security of their personal worlds.

Unlike fast-paced people, slower-paced individuals communicate by asking more "Why?" "How?" and "What do you mean by...?" kinds of questions. They keep their opinions to themselves and make tentative statements. They listen more than talk.

### PERSONAL SURVEY: PACE

Here are some statements to help you think through whether you tend to be a fast or slow-paced person. Circle one number in each pair that you feel is most like you.

1. I usually make up my mind quickly. *Or...*
2. I like to take my time in decision-making.

3. I tend to speak quickly and with emphatic statements. *Or...*
4. I tend to speak more slowly and with less-emphatic statements.

5. I find it hard to sit and do nothing. *Or...*
6. I enjoy quiet, do-nothing times.

7. I consider myself to have an active lifestyle. *Or...*
8. I consider myself to have a more low-key lifestyle.

9. I tend to be energized by juggling several balls at once. *Or...*
10. I prefer to do one thing at a time.

11. I easily become impatient with slower people. *Or...*
12. I do not like to be rushed.

13. I am quick to tell someone what I think or feel. *Or...*
14. I am more private about what I think and feel.

15. I like taking chances and trying new and different things. *Or...*
16. I do not like to take chances. I like familiar ways of doing things.

17. I tend to introduce myself at social gatherings. *Or...*
18. I am more likely to wait to be introduced at social gatherings.

19. When others talk, I have difficulty listening. *Or...*
20. When others talk, I listen carefully.

21. I like to be in charge. *Or...*
22. I prefer to follow directions and be supportive.

23. I tend to react more quickly and spontaneously. *Or...*
24. I tend to react more slowly and deliberately.

Now go back and determine whether you circled more even- or odd-numbered statements. If you circled more odd numbered statements, you tend to be more fast-paced. The even numbered statements describe a slow-paced person. Record your totals below:

_______ (#Odd/Fast-Paced)
_______ (#Even/Slower-Paced)

Many parents feel some confusion when I talk about fast and slow pace, because they find parenting to be a fast-paced activity, especially once the children pass the toddler stage. Moms and dads hustle their kids from school to soccer games, from homework to piano lessons, from one chore to the grocery store. And then they dash out to their own activities and responsibilities. There just doesn't seem to be enough hours in the day to get it all done.

Don't equate the fast pace of parenting with the speed I'm talking about here, however—that of your internal motor. One way to understand the difference is to answer the following questions: When you are forced to operate at a fast pace, do you feel comfortable or hurried? Do you feel re-energized or rushed? When slow-paced people are forced into fast-paced activities (including parenting), they often feel emotionally and physically drained at the end of a busy day. Fast-paced people thrive on activity and feel stress when they're forced to slow down.

## TASK-ORIENTED, PEOPLE-ORIENTED

The second strand in our tapestry, horizontal this time, I call *priority*. Priority is your *focus*—the motivation behind your movement. If pace is your internal *motor*, priority is your internal *compass*, which gives you direction.

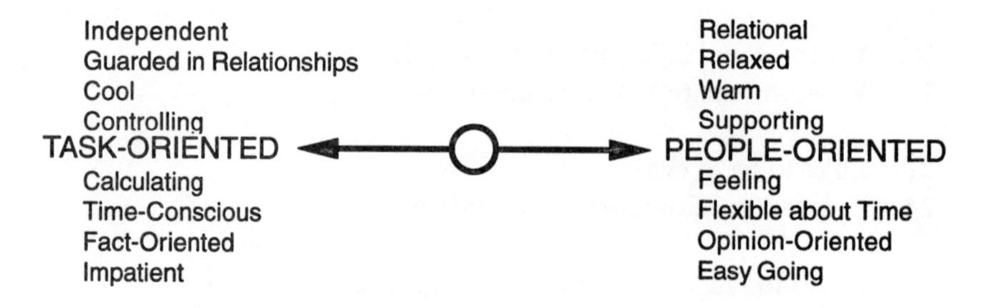


(The above diagram is derived from *The Family Discovery Profile Manual.*[2])

The daily actions of some individuals are task-oriented; others are more people-oriented. Again, we're not talking good or bad, just different. All types of individuals are needed in the fabric of society.

*Task-oriented* people focus on "doing things." They plan their work and work their plan. They stick with their own agenda. They often prefer to work alone—that way things are done the way they want.

They base their decisions on facts and data, as opposed to opinions and feelings. The tend to talk more about work and acquiring things than about people. When they do talk about people, they often seek to solve problems rather than understand them.

They also tend to be more guarded and aloof in their relationships. They like to keep their distance and may, at first meeting, be perceived by others as being cool, rather than warm. They have a strong sense of personal space and territory, so they don't touch you and you don't touch them. They tend to come across as more formal and proper, hiding their personal feelings. Small talk does not come easily for them.

*People-oriented* folks focus on "being *with* people." They come across as relaxed, warm, and responsive. They are energized by sharing and caring. They tend to be informal and personable, and not as concerned if things are out of place or are not done on time.

They are sensitive to the feelings of others and sensitive to what others say or do to them. They share their feelings easily. You never have to wonder how they feel because you can see it in their eyes and face—through nonverbal communication.

Since they focus more on relationships than tasks, they make it easy for you to know them. They share life experiences and use more subjective, feelings-oriented words and expressions. They like to tell stories and may frequently wander off the topic of conversation.

Karen and I recently visited a couple in their new home. The house had been completed less than three months but it already had a very "lived in" look. We walked in the door; toys were scattered all over the floor and things were out of place.

Our friends, however, were warm and cordial and made us feel right at home. We had a wonderful time. They didn't make apologies for how the house looked; in fact, they didn't even see the house as being "messy." Why? Because they made people a higher priority than picking up toys and straightening things up.

I also think of our good friends, Doug and Patty. When they attend one of their son's soccer games, you see their orientations emerge. Doug is more task-oriented, and he goes to watch the game. Patty goes to be with people. She moves up and down the stands from person to person, catching up on what's going on in their lives. And she seldom misses much of the game, either. Her antenna is wired to pick up both how her son and *everyone else* is doing.

### PERSONAL SURVEY: PRIORITY

Below are statements to help you think through your priority focus. Again, circle one statement in each pair that you feel best describes you.

1. I approach life in a serious manner. *Or...*
2. I approach life in a playful manner.

3. I tend to keep my feelings to myself. *Or...*
4. I tend to share my feelings with others.

5. I enjoy talking about and listening to facts and data. *Or...*
6. I enjoy telling and listening to stories about people.

7. I tend to make decisions based on facts, objectives, or evidence. *Or...*
8. I tend to make decisions based on feelings, experiences, or relationships.

9. I tend to be less interested in small talk. *Or...*
10. I tend to be more interested in small talk.

11. I maintain control over who I get to know and who I am involved with. *Or...*
12. I am more open to establishing new relationships and getting to know people better.

13. People may perceive me as being a little hard to get to know. *Or...*
14. People tend to perceive me as easy to get to know.

15. I prefer to work independently and alone. *Or...*
16. I prefer to work with and through others.

17. I discuss current issues and the tasks at hand. *Or...*
18. I like to talk about people, stories, and anecdotes.

19. I think of myself as a more formal person. *Or...*
20. I think of myself as a more casual person.

21. Other people view me as a thinker. *Or...*
22. Other people see me as a feeler.

23. I feel best when I am accomplishing something. *Or...*
24. I feel best when I am accepted by others.

If you circled more odd numbered statements, you tend to be more task-oriented. If you circled more even numbers, you are more people-oriented. Total the number of odd and even responses in the blanks below.

_______ (#Odd/Task-Oriented)
_______ (#Even/People-Oriented)

Before I move on, I should note that the descriptive phrases I've used throughout this discussion on pace and priority are *tendencies*. Generally, people fall into these categories, but not always. For example, I *tend* to make quick decisions, but I do not *always* make quick decisions. I am not a slave to this characteristic—I do have a choice—but it is generally true for me.

John Mark under his wing. Each had different priorities, and God's work was accomplished. Paul went on to have a fruitful ministry, planting churches and advancing the Christian faith, and later we learn that John Mark was restored.

## KNITTING THE STRANDS TOGETHER

Once you understand these two strands—"fast-paced/slow-paced" and "task-oriented/people-oriented"—the next step is to see how they combine to form different behavioral styles.

Note that when you place the two strands together on the same chart, you form four distinct quadrants, each signifying a different behavioral style. This is called the "DISC" model of understanding human behavior.

Let me translate this for you:

People (parents or children) who are fast-paced and task-oriented fall into the **"D,"** or **directive/determined** behavioral style. Generally, they are dominant, decisive, and often demanding. They like to be in control, and they are motivated to overcome any opposition or obstacle which stands between them and their goal.

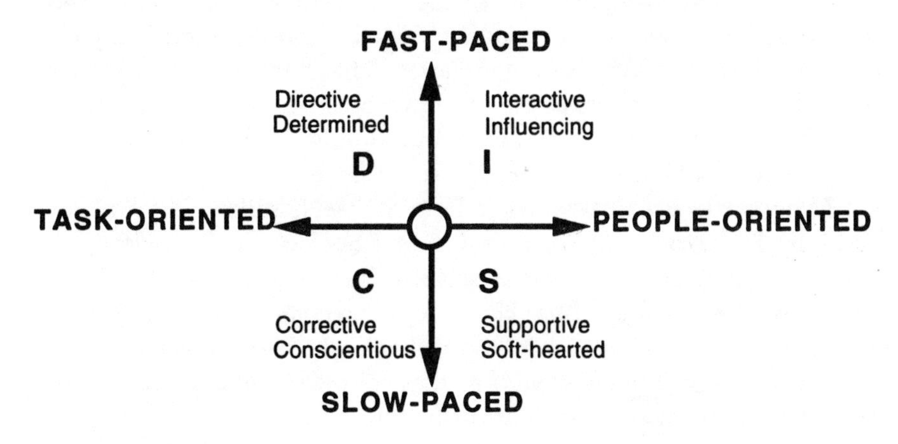


Fast-paced, people-oriented people generally have the **"I"** or **interactive/influencing** style. They also want things to go their way, but they do it differently from the "D's." They take charge, not by direct action, but by *persuading* others to go along with their ideas. They are warm, enthusiastic individuals whom others enjoy being with.

Those who are slow-paced and people-oriented fit the **"S"** or **supportive/soft-hearted** category. They are easygoing, dependable, and prefer things to remain the same. They usually adapt to what is going on around them rather than lead. They cooperate with others and are most comfortable in favorable, supportive situations.

Finally, slow-paced and task-oriented people can be described as **"C"** or **corrective/conscientious** individuals. They like things done the "right" or "correct" way, *as they see it.* They have analytical minds, they often are formal and reserved, and they are well-organized.

It's interesting to note that different people throughout history have come up with similar systems to explain the variations they see in people. In fact, many have used four categories. Hippocrates, the father of modern medicine, believed personality was shaped by different types of body fluid. He espoused four basic temperaments: Choleric (black bile), Sanguine (blood), Phlegmatic (phlegm), and Melancholy (yellow bile). Authors such as Tim LaHaye have applied a similar system in a variety of different books.

The DISC model (dominant, influencing, steady, compliant) traces its roots back to the work of Dr. William Moulton Marston. Most of my training in the DISC model has come through the profiles published by Carlson Learning Company. Their DiSC™ system[3] is based on Marston's theory and ongoing research conducted by Carlson Learning Company. Carlson's *Performax Personal Profile System®* has been used internationally for the past thirty years in the corporate business world as an aid to team building, management, leadership, communication enhancement, and conflict resolution.

Many books use this system to help counsel families. Gary Smalley and John Trent, for example, have written a book called *Two Sides of Love,* using animals (lion, otter, golden retriever, beaver) to explain the DISC styles. Another Smalley/Trent book I highly recommend is *The Treasure Tree,* a beautifully illustrated children's book which explains the strengths of each behavioral style so that your kids can understand how people are alike and how they are different.

### A PERSONAL TESTIMONY

Outside of God's Word, the insights I've gained through the DISC model are the most important body of information I possess. It has helped me understand where I best fit in the ministry, it has influenced my marriage (I'll share more about this later), and it is helping me apply Proverbs 22:6 in practical, specific ways. (Hence, this book!)

Some people distrust models like DISC because they feel it's wrong to "put labels" on anyone. I understand this concern. However, my experience is that understanding your behavioral style actually helps set you free to be who God created you to be.

Besides, I have yet to meet a person who does not "put labels" on people. When you meet someone, for example, you make a quick evaluation of him. In the space of a few seconds, you size up his looks, his personality, his intelligence, and how he makes you feel. If you're mature, you'll adjust your evaluation as you get to know this person, but chances are good that your initial impression will be difficult to shake. That's just human nature.

I think a greater problem is the large number of people who don't like themselves because they lack the ability to live up to others' expectations of how they should behave. Children sometimes develop a poor self-image because they sense their parents want them to act differently. A talented worker feels frustration because he cannot please a boss who doesn't understand his behavior and is more concerned with how he acts than with how he helps the company.

For many years, I felt boxed in by the expectations of other people and the particular denominational ideal of what a pastor was supposed to look and act like. In my first churches, it seemed as if people wanted me to keep things the same, stay within the routines. Subconsciously I "stuffed" major parts of who I was in order to fit. But I was not happy.

Once I understood my behavioral style, it gave me the confidence to decide I was going to behave the way God had designed me and not according to the expectations of others. I realized I needed an environment that was faster-paced, that gave me the opportunity to experiment and try new things. My DISC profile helps me know who I am and how to explain who I am to others. Like my name, "Boyd," it puts me in a *family* that I don't mind being associated with. It helps to *define* me, not *confine* me.

I am free to act in any way I choose. And some situations *do* call for me to move out of my comfort zone and use patterns of behavior that better meet the needs of others, or the needs of the moment, than does my "natural" style. But I'm still free to be me.

## PLOTTING YOUR SCORES

In the following chapters, I'll give you more information about the D, I, S, and C behavioral styles, and I'll help you determine your style and that of your child. For now, however, you can get a ballpark idea by using your scores from the pace and priority exercises you completed earlier in this chapter.

On the chart, mark with an "x" your *highest* pace score. Do the same for your *highest* priority score. Then draw a vertical line through the "x" on the fast-/slow-pace continuum and a horizontal line through the "x" on the task/people priority continuum. The point at which those two lines intersect will give you an indication of which quadrant and primary style you tend to be.

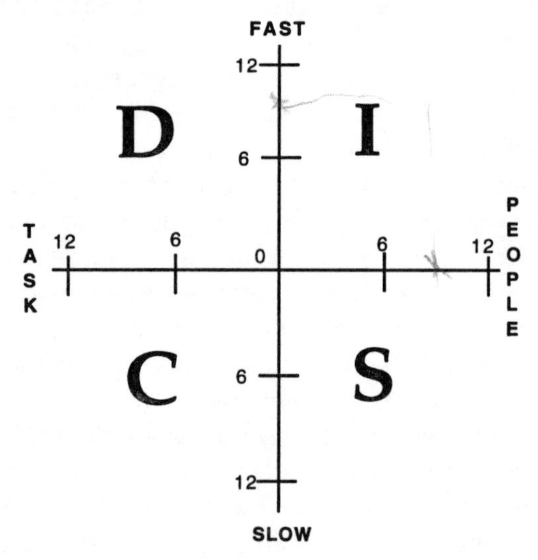


For example, if your pace totals were: Fast = 2 and Slow = 10, you would place an "x" on the Slow end *only* at 10. If your priority totals were: Task = 3 and People = 9, you would place an "x" on the People side *only* at 9. By extending a horizontal and vertical line from those points your lines would intersect in the "S" quadrant. If you come out 6 and 6 on either pace or priority, that would simply mean that you express equal amounts of both of those two styles of behaviors.

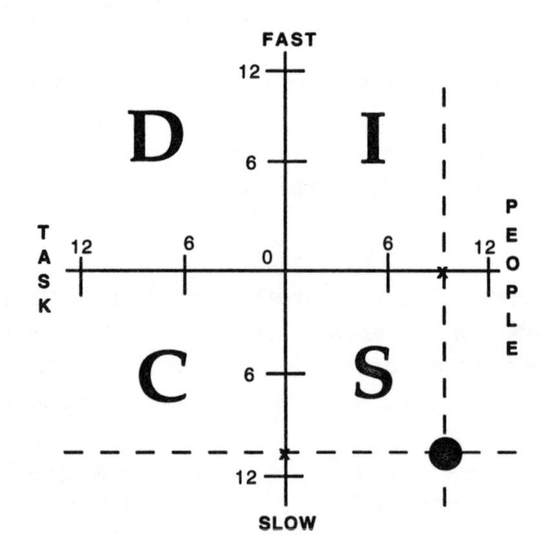

This simple system provides you with an excellent tool for getting a quick "read" on yourself and other people. However, this is only a "thumbnail sketch." You'll learn more in the next few chapters about each primary style.

It's also important to note that *each individual is a unique combination of each style*. For example, I am a high "D," but I also express a fair amount of "I" and "C" styles. My wife, Karen, scores highest in "C," but also is a strong "S."

Also, people may behave in different ways in different situations. For instance, a woman who is a high "D" in a work environment may exhibit more "I" behavior at home as a mother. A father who utilizes more of a high "C" style in parenting may express more "S" behavior at work.

Therefore, I strongly recommend that you obtain one or more of the Carlson Learning Company Profiles for a more accurate and in-depth understanding of your behavior style. Check the "Recommended Resources" section at the back of the book for more information on these helpful assessments.

## Bring Parenting Into Focus

As you read additional information about the DISC behavioral styles in the next four chapters, you will discover even more about your own and your children's unique behavioral styles. Much of what you read today on the subject of child-raising focuses on how to get your children to do things differently or more responsibly. Certainly, children do need to learn appropriate behavior. They do need to grow to become responsible adults.

I believe, though, that the more you understand yourself and your child, the better you'll be able to adapt the way you relate to him. And that will make you more successful at helping him become the person God wants him to be.

## Notes

1. Charles F. Boyd, *The Family Discovery Profile Manual* (Minneapolis: Carlson Learning Company), 8.

2. Boyd, *Family Profile*, 9.

3. DiSC™ is the distinctive trademark of Carlson Learning Company.

CHAPTER FOUR

# THE "D" STYLE

## DIRECTIVE PARENTS, DETERMINED CHILDREN

Can you imagine how the apostle Paul behaved as a child?

I can just picture him at age six—demanding to get his own way, unable to take no for an answer, wearing down his parents with his constant demands and desire to be in control. They probably echoed the lament I've heard from parents of kids like that: "I know that these qualities may serve him well in the future. But right now he's driving us crazy!"

Paul is a good example of what I introduced as the directive/determined behavioral style in the last chapter. As an adult, Paul exhibited a lot of "D" behavior. Before he became a Christian, he was dogmatic, decisive, determined, and demanding. He was a doer, a man on a mission to stamp out Christianity.

After his conversion, Paul's temperament didn't change, but God gave him a new mission. Now he was dedicated to telling people about Jesus Christ. During the next few decades he became one of the greatest, most dynamic leaders of the new Church.

I find it amusing to read what God did to capture Paul's attention and turn his life around so dramatically. God directly confronted him on the Damascus road, knocking him to his knees. Sometimes that's the only way to get a "D" to listen!

God talked straight to Paul. He said he would be an important man who would stand before kings and he would be used to turn people from darkness to light—exactly what a "D" likes to hear.

God also told Paul that he would suffer greatly in his ministry. High "D" individuals would find that energizing—they thrive on risk and challenge. Throughout Paul's ministry, that's exactly what he did. He persevered against all odds, overcoming all obstacles to proclaim the gospel.

Paul's divine training program included several stints in prison, and a "D" despises inactivity. I can imagine the inner struggles Paul went through before he was able to write in Philippians 4:12, "I have learned the secret of being content in any and every situation."

Sitting in a cold, dark prison cell, Paul had to believe God would make good on His promise to use him in a significant way, even if all he was doing was writing letters to churches. Today, of course, we know those letters as Paul's Epistles: eternal, Spirit-inspired words which provide guidance and encouragement for every believer.

Just as He did with Paul, our heavenly Father deals with us according to how He has designed us. He doesn't change our bents. Instead, He wants to use them for His glory. He arranges a personalized training program for us, divinely planned to complement our designs.

In the last chapter, I introduced the four primary behavioral styles. To help you discern your primary style and those of your children, I will examine each of the four more closely, beginning in this chapter with the "D" or directive/determined style. I'll present some specific examples of how the behavioral styles look in parents and children, and I'll give you some tips on how to work with kids who display each style.

## SEVEN PROMINENT CHARACTERISTICS OF THE DIRECTIVE/DETERMINED STYLE

High "D" people usually display many of the following qualities. If you want more information, or if you think this may be your primary behavioral style, look at the section headed, "Are You a 'D'?" at the end of this chapter.

- High Self-Confidence: They believe in themselves and their abilities. They are independent doers and thinkers and seldom require outside reassurance or advice. They make decisions quickly and easily. They can take care of themselves.
- Courageous: To live is to dare. They are risk-takers and adventure seekers. They are physically tough and will stand up to anyone who tries to take advantage of them.
- Results-oriented: High "D's" are ambitious and goal-oriented. They take a practical, pragmatic approach to accomplishing their objectives. They do what is necessary to get the job done. They tend to be easily angered and become impatient when their goals are blocked and potential results are jeopardized.
- Commanding: They aggressively take charge and enjoy giving orders. Theirs is an "I lead, you follow," "My way or the highway" approach to life. They expect everyone to understand that they are in charge and that their authority should be respected.

• Competitive: They assert themselves physically and often participate in sports. To the high "D," everything—work, play, and relationships—is viewed as winning or losing. They must be challenged or they will be bored. They are not easily discouraged and refuse to give up.

• Change-agent: Because they tend to be quick decision-makers, they frequently instigate new rules or procedures and often do so without consulting those who are affected by the changes.

• Direct, Straightforward: They communicate directly and to the point. Others may view them as blunt, tactless, harsh, or insensitive. Also, they prefer direct communication. They want to hear the bottom line rather than a long-winded story or a detailed explanation.

## THE DIRECTIVE PARENT

As a mom, Julie shows the same drive and enthusiasm as she once demonstrated in her work as an office manager. She is organized, purposeful, and energetic, and she expects to raise successful children who will turn out to be leaders themselves.

Julie sets strict rules for behavior in the house, and she expects her kids to obey her. If they don't, they receive swift discipline. She doesn't like to explain herself; she expects her children to do as she says, keep their word, and respect deadlines.

Here's how Julie describes herself: "As a parent, I know I can be too tough at times, but I think I'm fair. The problem is that kids today get away with too much. I believe that children should carry their fair share of the load at home. When they don't, I quickly correct the situation. I expect my children to obey me, and I take it very seriously if they don't.

"I love my children, and I believe that by expecting them to be responsible and hard-working, they will grow up knowing that I love them."

Directive parents provide a strong, capable role model to their children. They set high goals for themselves and are able to push themselves to achieve those goals. Kids know they can count on "D" parents for leadership and protection. They often are proud of their parent's accomplishments and success.

"D" parents are responsible, competent, and full of energy. They're good at getting things done and at directing their kids to help do it. When things go wrong, they continue to work toward meeting their goals.

They are actually energized by conflict. They love a good argument because it is something to overcome and win.

## HOW GOD MODELS THE "D" STYLE

Our heavenly Father models all four of the DISC parenting styles I will present in this book. We see the Directive parenting style in Psalm 32:8: "I will instruct you and teach you in the way you should go; I will counsel you and watch over you."

God gives specific directions for His children to follow. As the Creator, He's designed how life is to work. He also gives us directives to follow in order to maintain proper respect for His person and His truth. The Ten Commandments in the Old Testament, the Sermon on the Mount in the New Testament, and other passages throughout the Bible set forth in clearly defined terms what God expects from His children.

His commands demonstrate His love for us. When we live by His truth, we can be assured of maintaining an intimate relationship with Him. As His children, the proper response to His directing style is respect and obedience.

## INEFFECTIVE "D" PARENTS

While Directive parents have many positive qualities, in certain situations a negative side can emerge. In particular, when their children question their authority or assert independence, "D" parents may feel threatened and become autocratic.

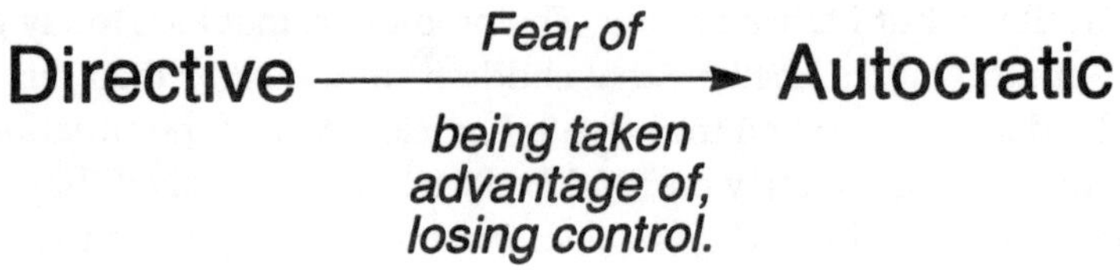

Often the greatest fear of Directive parents is that their children will take advantage of them. That fear can be the "hot button" that pushes them to be impatient, hot-tempered, and demanding. And since they are task-oriented, they also can appear to be aloof and cold.

Autocratic parents are drill sergeants who have one rule and one rule only: "As long as you live under my roof, you will do things my way."

You will hear this "prime directive" in a number of ways, but always with an exclamation point:

- "You'll do it because I say so, and that's that!"
- "Don't you dare talk back to me!"
- "Obey, or else!"

- "Don't ask why, just do it!"
- "I don't care how many of your friends will be there. You are not going and that's final!"
- "I'm sick and tired of your goofing off. We all have jobs to do around here and you will do your part!"

Autocratic parents must be in control of their children, and being in control means making all the decisions. They demand instant obedience and compliance to their rules.

They tend to use anger to control their children's behavior. They often push their children too hard. Their kids frequently complain, "You're always rushing me," or "You just don't understand me."

They tend to overuse parental authority in trying to get their children to conform to their wishes. Any kind of disagreement, especially lengthy explanations, is considered disrespectful.

These parents find it hard to admit when they are wrong. They are selective listeners, hearing only what they want to hear in order to correct situations and move on.

This "my way or the highway" approach may work in the business world, but at home it can have a long-lasting, negative impact on youngsters.

Children coming from these homes rank lowest in self-respect. Depending on a child's behavioral style, she may respond to rigidity and harshness in the home by stuffing her feelings and becoming passive-aggressive or loud, demanding, and actively rebellious. In school, she may be disruptive in order to gain attention. She may abuse drugs and become involved in illegal activities.

Make no mistake about it. Children raised in homes with an autocratic atmosphere are keeping score. Their anger and hurt is building up inside, and some day it will come out.

Many autocratic parents have a difficult time adjusting to their children becoming adults. They feel the need to keep on telling their children what to do and how to improve—even when those children are in their fifties.

"We fight every time I see her," says one grown woman of her mother. "If I'm there a week, we'll have two or three different battles.

"She always thinks she's right. She'll make some sort of abrasive comment, and if I say anything back, she'll attack me and try to invalidate my feelings.

"Recently she objected to the music I was listening to. I asked, 'Why are you so angry?'

" 'I'm not angry!' she replied.

" 'But Mom, you look angry, and you're acting angry.'

" 'Well, that's *your* problem!' "

## WHAT AUTOCRATIC PARENTS NEED

If you are a directive parent who tends to become autocratic, you need to work on listening, compromising, expressing more affection, and spending more time with your children. You need to have more fun, relax, listen, and be more sensitive to other people's feelings.

- As to control: Accept not being in charge all the time. Realize that you need to get things done with and through other people, and that they will stop responding to your leadership if it is not combined with a humble heart.
- As to communication: Be careful not to give answers too quickly. Explain yourself more, especially when you are directing your children to complete a task. Verbalize positive emotions. Allow others to ask questions without becoming defensive. Realize that others may be hurt or overwhelmed by the force and intensity of your comments and directives.
- As to pace: Resist becoming impatient with slower performance. Pace yourself to make sure there are family fun times when everybody, including you, can relax.
- As to priority: Give more attention to your relationships. Focus on your children as people, not just on their performance.
- As to spirituality: Openly admit when you are wrong and have made mistakes. Demonstrate humility by asking forgiveness.

## THE DETERMINED CHILD

It doesn't matter if you are nine, nineteen, thirty-nine, or fifty-nine. "D" behavior is "D" behavior. Only the arenas change. The seven general characteristics of the dominant style also apply to the "D" child, though the different character strengths may be in an early stage of development.

Mark and Jenny have no doubt that they are parents of a Determined child. Listen to their descriptions of their son, David:

"He's a very forceful kid. He tries to be in control of every situation, whether it's at the pool, dinner, playtime.

"The other day we were at the grocery store, and I was trying to pick out what type of peanut butter to buy. David became impatient and finally said, 'Just pick one, Dad!' He wanted to make a decision, get to the result.

"He's always energetic, always intense, very active. He's good in school because he works hard to complete his tasks.

"He also loves to compete, but he hates to lose. He's a good soccer player, but he gets angry when the other team scores a goal. When we play games at home, he pouts if he doesn't win."

David is also difficult to discipline. "We really have to be direct with him. Our other child is so sensitive that her feelings are hurt when you look at her wrong, but we need to be strict and forceful with David."

Jenny is a high "I," an Interactive parent, and she says she often feels like she's being "plowed under" by David. "The other day I announced, 'David, we're going to the mall soon.'

" 'I want to watch a video now!' he said.

" 'No, you can't because we're leaving in just a few minutes.' He then proceeded to become a holy terror because he didn't get his way.

"I can be patient for just so long with him, and then I explode. It's always a tug of war."

"I come home from work," Mark chimes in, "and Jenny is just beaten, worn out. I know it's time for me to spend time with David!"

Perhaps what wears at Mark and Jenny the most is David's constant questioning. "It just wears us out," Mark says. "We don't really get a break. He's relentless. He will not take no for an answer. To him, the word no means, 'I haven't asked enough.'

"He even will sometimes come to me and say, 'Dad, I know you're going to say no, but do you think we could go get some ice cream tonight?' "

The Determined child is a natural leader and as a result can be extremely strong-willed. She thinks ahead, she senses when parents are most vulnerable, and then she attacks. She loudly and angrily declares her disapproval when things don't go her way.

Because she says what she thinks, she often hurts people's feelings. She can be blunt, even brutal. On top of that, she finds it difficult to say "I'm sorry."

She also feels an overwhelming need to be in control. This need for control is not an option, but a driving force in her life.

The Determined child is like the boy in the "Calvin and Hobbes" cartoon who declares, "I'm at peace with the world. I'm completely serene.... I've discovered my purpose in life.... I am here so everybody can do what I want."

And then he says, "Once everyone accepts it, they'll be serene, too."

### WORKING WITH A "D" CHILD

Here are some ways to help a "D" child reach her full potential:

• Provide her with responsibilities in which she can exercise some control and choices. The degree of responsibility should increase with the age and maturity of the child.

• Give her specific goals to work toward. If appropriate, take advantage of her competitive nature. For example, if your goal is for her to clean her room thoroughly once a week, turn the chore into a game in which she earns something special if she completes the task within a certain time period.

• Help her understand that, while it is wise to set goals and go after them, failure is a part of life and doesn't mean *she* is a failure.

• Help her slow down and know when and how to relax.

• Teach her to accept the importance of limits and boundaries, even when she disagrees with you.

• Use her past struggles to help teach her about compassion and understanding for others who may be experiencing hurt or disappointment.

• Give her as many choices as possible. For example, start getting her prepared for bedtime early by saying, "Would you like to go to bed now or when this show is over?"

• When it's time for action, use very brief commands. "Bedtime!" "Clean the room!"

• Since she has a high need for physical activity, provide many opportunities to run, jump, and be active. Avoid activities that require sitting for a long time.

• Above all, do not allow yourself to get pulled into a power struggle with your "D" child. When correcting her behavior, focus on actions and be specific as to what needs to be done. Reason with her sensibly and logically, but not at length. In an attempt to control the discipline, she may openly question the way things are done or attempt to negotiate for lesser punishment. Be brief and to the point. Let her know who's in charge.

I saw a good example of how to handle a Determined child one day at a restaurant. A dad walked in with two girls. He chose a table, but then noticed that his five-year-old girl was dragging a wooden highchair for her younger sister to a different table.

"Dana, over here," he said.

"No, Dad, this is a good table. Let's sit here."

"This table has just as much space and the highchair will work better here," he replied.

Dana continued to insist on the table she had chosen. This verbal battle raged on until the man finally went over, gently put one hand on Dana and the other on the highchair, and pushed them over to his table.

With that act, he established who was in control. But I have a feeling the battles still rage in that household. As they left at the end of their meal, I overheard Dana ask, "Dad, can I pick the table next time?"

## ARE YOU A HIGH "D"?

Below is a list of traits characteristic of the "D"-style individual. Think about your behavior and interactions with other people. Highlight those statements that you feel describe you:

I am able to make decisions quickly.

When I start a project, I finish it.

I have a lot of confidence in my skills.

I like to get right to the point when I talk with people, and I get impatient with people who like to tell long stories.

I like to set goals and work to achieve them.

I'm more interested in getting the job done than in making people like me.

I enjoy leading a project.

I get bored when I don't have something to keep me challenged.

I don't like anyone looking over my shoulder. I like the freedom to do my job *my* way.

I become aggressive and determined under pressure.

I tend to have a low amount of tolerance for the feelings and opinions of others.

I feel energized by a problem that needs to be solved.

I dislike the petty details when I'm working on a project. I'd rather delegate those to someone else while I look at the big picture.

I often project a cool, aloof style.

I love to compete, and I hate to lose.

CHAPTER FIVE

# THE "I" STYLE

## INTERACTIVE PARENTS, INFLUENCING CHILDREN

Suzanne was shopping with her grandmother when she noticed some little plastic watches selling for two dollars. "Oh, Grandma, please buy me a watch," Suzanne said. "I don't have a watch. I need a watch, Grandma. If you love me, you'll buy me a watch."

Her grandmother tried to reason with her, telling her that the cheap watches wouldn't last long. But Suzanne persisted and cajoled until...you guessed it. Few grandmas have the ability to withstand such a determined onslaught from a beloved grandchild.

The next morning Suzanne tried to wind the watch, and it broke. The grandmother thought, *This will be a great lesson for Suzanne.* She looked at the girl and said, "See, you should have listened to me. I told you the watch was cheap. If you had listened to me, we wouldn't have this problem."

Suzanne looked back at her grandmother and said, "I'm just a little kid. You should have made me listen to you!"

The grandmother later said, "She was so convincing, I didn't know what had happened or who was right. I stood there and apologized to her!"

As you can guess, Suzanne is a typical "I" individual. High "I's" demonstrate an interactive/influencing style and focus their energies on influencing and persuading others. They tend to be optimistic, talkative, and eager to please others. They seek social recognition, and they also are emotional—they let you know how they feel about things.

High "I's" are dynamic, more oriented to action than thought. They tend to decide quickly and move to action without much delay. They trust their feelings and make intuitive decisions based on how they feel.

They tend to generate enthusiasm and excitement in their interactions with others. They do not like doing things by themselves and will gravitate toward group activities and events.

## SEVEN PROMINENT CHARACTERISTICS OF THE INTERACTIVE/INFLUENCING STYLE

• People-oriented: High "I's" genuinely love people and are highly social. Their "prime directive" is to win friends and influence people. Their energy and enthusiasm inspire others to join in. Many are highly intuitive about other people's feelings and are skilled at reading people. They are trusting of others and tend to project unconditional acceptance toward a variety of people.

• Emotional: They tend to display their emotions freely and openly. They are animated, dramatic, and they react emotionally to people and events. Most are physically affectionate and need to receive plenty of love in return. On the flip side, they have a difficult time with emotional control and are often highly sensitive to any kind of personal criticism. They hate to be alone.

• Talkative: High "I's" are persuasive communicators and love to talk. They often tell colorful and entertaining stories and jokes.

• Fun Loving: These people are a party waiting to happen. They like to laugh and make others laugh. Because they make things happen, life is fast-paced for them, rarely dull or boring.

• Optimistic: Interactive people see the positive side of almost any situation. They anticipate the best and dismiss any possibility of failure. Their motto is: "Don't worry! Be happy!" They try to make the best of difficulties by sincerely believing that everything will work out. At the same time, they tend to cope with stress by ignoring unpleasant realities.

• Spontaneous: They enjoy a variety of activities, and need the freedom to follow their feelings and go with the flow. Being free spirited, they tend to be impulsive and disorganized. They dislike structured environments or anything that would limit their personal freedoms. The down side is that they are not natural planners. They tend to not follow through with details.

• Seek social acceptance and applause: High "I's" thrive on compliments, praise, and admiration. They like to be seen and noticed and tend to position themselves to be the center of attention. They come alive when all eyes are on them. Since they tend to define themselves from the outside in, their greatest fear is being rejected by others. Their self-portrait is painted by how other people see them. If you asked a high "I" to describe himself, you might hear: "My friends say I'm,..." or "Other people tell me...."

## A BIBLICAL EXAMPLE

Peter, one of Jesus' disciples, strikes me as core "I." Here was a man who was sure of himself, was the first to speak out in a group, and was extremely impulsive.

If you look at the amount of space given to the comments and questions of the twelve disciples in the Gospels, you'll find that Peter talks more than the other eleven combined. He was a man who spoke quickly and sometimes rashly. But his speeches in the Book of Acts and the style of his Epistles also reveal he was a gifted communicator, despite the fact that he had little formal education.

One night when the disciples were out in the boat, Jesus came to them, walking on the water. Who but Peter would have thought he could walk on water? Peter said, "Is that Jesus walking on the water? I want to walk on water, too!" Over the side he went. Peter always wanted to try new things.

He was also quick to speak. In Matthew 16 when Jesus asks the disciples, "Who do people say the Son of Man is?" Peter is the first to answer. His words, "You are the Christ, the Son of the living God," received the praise of Christ Himself. In just a few more verses, Jesus goes on to tell the disciples that He must go to Jerusalem and die. When Peter hears this, he again jumps in, "Never, Lord! This shall never happen to you!" And with that comment, Jesus replied, "Out of my sight, Satan!"

In Mark 14, when Jesus speaks of His coming death, Peter vows his undying loyalty. "Even if I have to die with you, I will never disown you," he declares (v. 31). But in "I"-like fashion, his follow-through was not so good. After Jesus' arrest, a servant girl accused Peter of being one of Jesus' followers. Peter cursed and repeatedly denied knowing the Lord.

After Jesus' crucifixion and resurrection, the disciples are in a boat, fishing, when Jesus comes and speaks to them from the shore. Peter recognizes immediately that He is the risen Christ, and again, over the side he went, as the rest rowed to shore.

Throughout the Bible, God used high "I's" to carry on His work. Who did Moses want to go with him to persuade Pharaoh to let the nation of Israel go? His high "I" brother, Aaron. Who did God establish as the king of Israel at a critical time in history? A high "I" after his heart, David. Who led the first-century church? Peter. And who encouraged discouraged disciples? Barnabas. All were high "I's" whom God used to persuade and influence His people to follow Him.[1]

## THE INTERACTIVE PARENT

There are two groups of people in the world: the huggers and the handshakers. Handshakers ("D"- and "C"-style folks for the most part) extend their hands with their arms stiff and outstretched to help you keep your distance. Huggers will embrace a perfect stranger. High "I's" are huggers in every sense of the word.

High "I" parents love to gather friends and their children together and talk, talk, talk. They love storytelling, wrestling, and of all parents, are the most free to play with their children.

They maintain a fast pace, seeking a variety of activities to keep themselves and their children entertained. They want to do things with their children.

Interactive parents project warmth and understanding; others turn to them when they have a problem. They become bored with details or with routine work like household cleaning. They'd rather do something with other people.

One Saturday afternoon I sat with my wife at our neighborhood swimming pool, describing the different types of parenting styles. As I talked, I noticed that a woman near Karen and me was looking right at us, listening in on our conversation.

All of a sudden, this woman jumped in to the conversation and didn't run out of breath for about five minutes: "You know those parenting styles you are talking about? Well, I'm the high 'I.' "

*No kidding?* I thought.

The woman went on. "You have described me perfectly. I love my children and I want to have fun with them. All through the summer I have arranged time for me and my two daughters to go on some adventure each week. Last week it was the zoo, this week we are going to an amusement park in Dallas, and next week, when my husband's out of town, I'm going to let each of them have two friends over and we are going to have the best slumber party you have seen!

"And you know what else you said that was interesting? I do have a really hard time with discipline. I just don't like to be the heavy in any situation. I want to be friends with my kids and I guess my fear is that they won't like me. Do you think that's wrong? I know that is probably too permissive. But I don't like saying no. Besides that, I want my kids to have all the things I never had growing up. I just want my kids to grow up and think back on our family as having been a fun, positive one to grow up in."

At this point, my eyes began to glaze over, like a deer staring into headlights.

I probably couldn't have found a better example of an "I" parent.

These individuals make home a warm and fun place. Their children never lack for affection.

### HOW GOD MODELS THE "I" STYLE

Our heavenly Father demonstrates an Interactive parenting style in His desire to be involved with His children. Many people mistakenly view God as distant and aloof. They have a God-is-watching-us-from-a-distance mentality.

It is astounding to think that the God of the universe wants us to know Him, that He has taken extraordinary measures to communicate that He wants to be part of our lives. In fact, that's the whole message of the Bible: God wants us to know Him personally.

In John 17:3 Jesus says, "Now this is eternal life: that they may know you, the only true God, and Jesus Christ, whom you have sent." The proper response to a God who invites you to know Him and enter into a personal relationship with Him, is to accept His invitation. We do that by faith in His Son, Jesus Christ.

### INEFFECTIVE "I" PARENTS

My acquaintance at the swimming pool mentioned the problem many "I" parents face: They want their children to like them and can't bear the thought of disapproval. Because of this, these parents can become overly permissive.

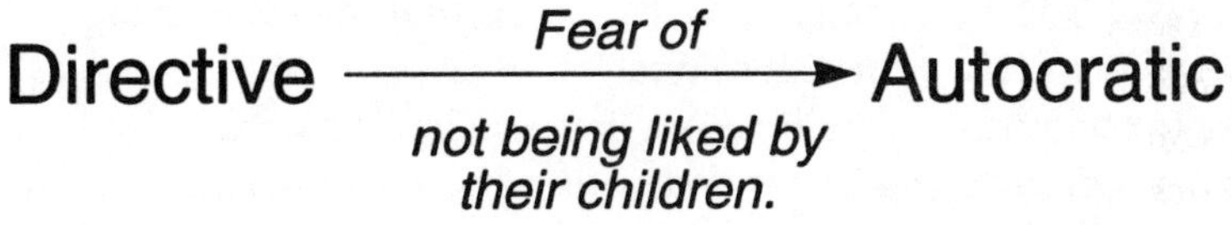

Directive —— *Fear of not being liked by their children.* ——→ Autocratic

Permissive parents want to do things for their children, but in the process they make the mistake of giving their children free reign. Their unspoken creed is, "I'll do whatever it takes to make them happy."

They dislike saying no to their children. When lines are crossed, they simply draw another line or ignore the problem and hope it will go away. They might even laugh off something that should be taken seriously.

While visiting a friend's home, I witnessed this scenario: A high "I" father noticed his young son, Seth, venturing out into the street. "Seth, do not go into the street," he said.

A few minutes later, Seth ran into the street again, and my friend said, "Seth, what did I tell you? Do not play in the street. It's dangerous." A few more minutes passed, then, "Seth, this is the last time I'm going to tell you. Don't go into the street." Then my friend looks over at me and says, "I just don't know what I'm going to do with that kid."

My friend needed to be more forceful. Talking to Seth wasn't going to keep him from playing in the street. This dad needed to take swift, decisive action and discipline Seth for disobeying him.

In 1 Samuel 2–3 we read about Eli, the high priest of Israel during the time of the judges. The text tells us that Eli's sons were stealing portions of the sacred sacrifices from the people. They were also sleeping with the women who served in the Temple. Eli heard about these things and confronted his sons, but they did not listen. Eli didn't take further action. Later, God revealed His judgment on Eli and his sons to young Samuel: "For I told him [Eli] that I would judge his family forever because of the sin he knew about; his sons made themselves contemptible, and he failed to restrain them" (1 Samuel 3:13).

Permissive parents also may tend to take what their children say at face value, refusing to probe and ask questions. They tend to see only the good in their children. They set themselves up to be manipulated.

The parenting philosophy of permissive parents is: Do whatever makes you happy. Do it any way *you* want. They do not want their children to be unhappy, especially with them. They also may fear that if they are too strict, they may damage their children in some way.

### WHAT PERMISSIVE PARENTS NEED

Interactive parents need to learn and apply some of the skills of the Directive ("D") and Corrective ("C") styles so that they do not slip into an ineffective, overly permissive style.

• As to communication: Be more firm in communicating limits and boundaries. Let your yes be yes and your no be no. Don't allow yourself to be pulled in to persuasive and persistent arguments. Don't feel like you must always explain why you want something done. Don't allow yourself to get sidetracked with lengthy stories. Get to the point and stick to the point.

Concentrate on listening more. Heart-to-heart talks require understanding what's in the heart of the other person. Keep yourself from exaggerating so that you don't become dishonest.

Also, be careful of taking what your children say at face value. Ask more questions to find out important details you might otherwise miss.

• As to pace: Slow down, especially if you have slower-paced children. Your pace can cause them a great degree of internal stress if you are not careful.

• As to permissiveness: Be aware of your difficulty with saying "no." A loving parent must take firm stands at times. Though your child may become upset with you, in the long run he will thank you for it.

• As to priority: Focus more on prioritizing and keeping commitments. One reason you may become permissive is that you want people to cut you slack if your own priorities slip, so you feel you must do the same for them.

Write down plans for following through on tasks and taking care of the details. Self-discipline gives you a platform for disciplining your children.

• As to spirituality: Remember, faith and positive, optimistic thinking are not the same thing. Confusing the two may result in unrealistic expectations for you and your family.

### THE INFLUENCING CHILD

Like high "I" parents, the Influencing child's goal in life is to have fun and enjoy people.

On one occasion, Karen and I invited our youth pastor, Brian, and his wife over for supper. Karen and our son, Chad, went to the grocery store to pick up a few items. As they passed an aisle containing some toys, Chad (a high "D" and a high "I") pulled out a whoopee cushion and said, "Hey, let's get this and put it under Brian's chair!"

Karen is a high "C," but knowing Chad had that "I" in him, she said, "Great, let's do it." She became part of the scheme, plotting right along with Chad as to how to make this trick work well.

High "I" children can also talk your ear off. That's how Esther is. She's at the age where the telephone is permanently attached to the side of her head. One day Esther's father heard her make some smart remarks to her mother. "Esther," he said, "I can understand how you feel, but you cannot talk to your mother like that." He put her on telephone restriction for a week.

Of course, preventing a high "I" from using the phone is like taking water away from a thirsty man. After one day, Esther said, "Daddy, could you just give me a spanking and get this over with? This phone restriction is killing me!"

Influencing children stay active, and want to stay active *with* other people. A friend who has a high "I" daughter remarks, "She can't stand to be alone. When I hear her say, 'I have nothing to do,' I know the real problem is that she doesn't have anyone to play with. In the same way, she hates to do housework unless my wife or I are doing it with her. Then it becomes fun."

These kids are full of wonderful, creative ideas but are often defeated in carrying them out because of a short attention span. "He's a live wire," or "She can't sit still for one minute," are frequent descriptions of "I" children. They tend to act on impulse and think later.

They trust other people. Nobody is a stranger; everyone is their best friend.

They are extremely sensitive to what other kids think of them, so they're especially vulnerable to peer pressure. They like people and want to be liked. Acceptance by their peers can become an obsession.

Their loving nature can change to immediate anger when something or someone crosses them. Their emotions are combinations of highs and lows, going from laughter to tears and back to laughter. Because of their quick-changing moods, they readily adjust to disappointments and usually make the best of a bad situation.

Influencing children are open with their feelings and need lots of hugging and kissing. Chad has a lot of "I" in him, and every night I go up and lie down right on top of him—a full body-press. We wrestle around a minute or two and have our prayers together. Then he gives me a big bear hug and kiss. He may not act like he enjoys this in front of his friends, but when it's just the two of us at bed time, he won't go to sleep without it.

### WORKING WITH AN "I" CHILD

Here are ways you can help an "I" child reach his full potential:

• Plan for fun times. Make your home a warm, friendly place to be.

• Give constant encouragement. Be specific in describing his strengths and accomplishments. (There will be more on this in later chapters.)

• Put instructions in writing. Provide ideas for transferring talk into action.

• Dream with your child. Let your imagination run wild with his as you fantasize about things to do, places to go—even if you cannot possibly make the dream come true. Just say, "It would be great if our whole family could go to Hawaii together. What would you do first if we could go?" Let him dream without feeling you have to bring him back to reality.

• Immediately reward him when he does something good by giving special incentives and recognition—such as gold stars, awards, and ribbons.

• Give lots of hugs and kisses. He needs large doses of consistent affection.

• Understand that he wants to do what everybody else is doing. Help him be firm and direct in dealing with peer pressure and unfavorable situations.

• Help him think through the details of a project.

• Don't be cool, aloof, distant, impersonal, too task-oriented, or tight-lipped. He will conclude that you think something is wrong with him or that you don't like him.

• Don't be critical or judgmental. Never put him down in public, especially in front of his friends.

• Make sure your "I" child has friends to play with, and take advantage of his desire for companionship by doing things with him, especially during the preteen years when he wants to be with you!

## ARE YOU A HIGH "I"?

Below is a list of traits characteristic of the "I"-style individual. Think about your behavior and interactions with other people. Highlight those statements that you feel describe you:

I like to talk. I'm never at a loss for words.
I feel comfortable at large parties.
I usually have no problem talking with new people.
I like being involved in a project as long as I'm doing it with someone else.
I'm able to persuade others to join me in different activities and projects.
Being with other people energizes me. I dislike being alone for too long.
I always seem to be able to jump into activities with great enthusiasm.
I generally like to look at the positive side of things.
People have little problem guessing how I'm feeling.
I have little trouble expressing what I think about things.
I enjoy being up front in a large group; I like the recognition.
I have a lot of friends.
I'm not always as organized as I should be.
Sometimes I have a problem completing a project; I tend to jump from one activity to another.
I like doing things differently. I'm able to come up with creative and imaginative ideas.

## NOTE

1. For more on how the DISC model can help you understand Bible characters, see Ken Voges and Ron Braund, *Understanding How Others Misunderstand You* (Chicago: Moody Press, 1990). Ken has also written *The Biblical Personal Profile* (Minneapolis: Carlson Learning Company) that will help you compare your behavioral style to that of selected men and women of the Bible. For more information, see the resource list in Appendix C.

CHAPTER SIX

# THE "S" STYLE

## SUPPORTIVE PARENTS, SOFT-HEARTED CHILDREN

Cats. It was the way Buck played with cats that convinced Barbara that he would make a good father. "Just the way he showed affection with them—he had a calm, gentle quality."

There was more to Buck, though. "He's steady. He's there for you. Dependable."

And affectionate. Barbara grew up in a family which did not openly express feelings, and when Buck first began saying, "I love you," she couldn't say it back. "I wanted him to quit saying 'I love you' so much!" she says.

You probably know people like Buck. High "S" individuals like him are the steady ones, the "rocks" who help set the emotional tone of a home or an office. You feel comfortable around them.

### SEVEN PROMINENT CHARACTERISTICS OF THE SUPPORTIVE/SOFT-HEARTED STYLE

• Steadfast: They will stick with you through thick and thin. They are long suffering, devoted, and loyal. They also stick to a task until it is done and are remarkably consistent for their ages. When this positive strength is taken to an extreme, they can also become very set in their ways.

• Team player: At their best, people with this style are devoted, considerate, and committed to the team, whether that team be family- or work-related. They are cooperative and prefer not to make decisions that might upset the status quo.

• Prefer familiarity: Because they need the security of structure and routine, they want things done at regular times and in consistent order. They are most comfortable with established habit patterns and repetition. They do not like unplanned change or surprises, and need plenty of time to adjust when change is inevitable. They dislike change because it threatens their security, and they will at times stubbornly persist in trying to keep things as they are. They place a great deal of importance on stability within their family.

• Render service: The "prime directive" of the high "S" is to be helpful to others. They do not wait to be asked. Their happiness comes from meeting the needs of others. Most often, they would rather follow than lead.

• Humble: They do not like being in the spotlight or the center of attention. They do not boast about their accomplishments, and even though they need to feel appreciated, they do not like to be fussed over. They take care to maintain a courteous, restrained, yet friendly demeanor. They do not want to appear proud or pushy, and they are uncomfortable with too much positive attention, especially in public.

• Committed to people: They tend to be easygoing and warm in their relationships with other people. They strive to maintain harmony by tolerating other people's mistakes, and they are seldom harsh when they correct those mistakes. They may not have as many friends as an "I," but they are loyal and committed to the ones they have. They are the ones who have a wallet full of family pictures. They cultivate close, lasting relationships.

• Pragmatic: Theirs is a step-by-step, practical approach to accomplishing tasks. They tend to think before they act and need to know how something is to be done from start to finish. Because of their orientation toward practical action and thought, most people describe them as easy to live and work with.

High "S" individuals have natural counseling skills and are extremely supportive. They are compassionate and good listeners. They also make good diplomats and peacemakers.

They dislike pushy, aggressive behavior and are bothered by impersonal approaches. Their main question is, "How will what you are proposing affect me, my work, my family, my life?"

Their greatest strength is that they are dependable, supportive, and cooperative. The greatest weakness is that people can take advantage of them. They can be overly sensitive. They may not be willing to change when change is in their best interest.

### A Biblical Example

Scripture presents Abraham as a man who expressed many high "S" traits. Genesis 13, for example, describes how he settled with his wife, Sarah, and his nephew, Lot, in a place called Bethel. Because both men had large herds, it was difficult for them to stay together without frequent feuds between Abraham's herdsmen and the herdsmen of Lot. So

Abraham, the peacemaker, steps in and says, "Let's not have any quarreling between you and me, or between your herdsmen and mine, for we are brothers. Is not the whole land before you? Let's part company. If you go to the left, I'll go to the right; if you go to the right, I'll go to the left" (vv. 8-9).

Now let me ask you: How would a high "D" like the apostle Paul have handled that situation? "Look, Lot, *you* are traveling with *me*, remember? I'm in charge. I'm doing you a favor by letting you come along. You need to keep your flocks and herds away from mine. So talk to your men and keep them in line—or else!"

But Abraham was willing to allow Lot first choice of whatever land he wanted. Lot chose what he considered to be the best land—the lush, green, well-watered land of the Jordan, Sodom and Gomorrah—and he set out east. Abraham made no major changes. He continued to live in Canaan. That's just like an "S"—wanting to make peace, and wanting the best for everyone involved in the dispute.

### THE SUPPORTIVE PARENT

High "S's" provide a strong sense of security for their children. They are tuned into meeting their needs, often at their own expense. They tend to be extremely nurturing, especially when their children are babies. They are attentive to their children and watchful of their safety.

They give their children a strong sense of home and family. They help create a warm, comfortable, supportive home environment centered around people and familiar routines. They also are good at establishing family traditions.

A classic example of a high "S" mother was Edith Bunker. If you overlook the ditzy side of her character that Archie continually put down, Edith was the stabilizing factor in that family. Even though Archie clashed with the Meathead, Edith got along with both of them.

In his book *People Smart*, author Tony Alessandra called her "*A Bridge over Troubled Water*, the heart of the family unit."[1] She genuinely enjoyed her family and neighbors (even George Jefferson), despite their differences. She focused on everyone's positive qualities and didn't seem to notice the negatives. She personified the considerate, neighborly, and predictable behaviors of the "S" style.[2]

I grew up with an "S" mother. Her home and family were her highest priority. She was loving, caring, and very sensitive to both my needs and the needs of my father. She was not a risk taker, but preferred to keep things on an even keel. I remember our home as a safe, peaceful place in which to grow up. Our evenings were spent sitting together, enjoying each other's company in calm and quiet.

Mom also loved to serve people—it was her gift. She particularly enjoyed trying to think about what you needed before you realized you wanted it. If Dad and I were sitting in the family room watching television, she would say, "Would anyone like something to drink?"

"Well," I would say, "now that I think about it, a Dr. Pepper would be nice about now." And before we could look up from that episode of "Combat" or "Dr. Kildare," she would hand each of us a cold glass full of D.P. She waited on us hand and foot.

And today…my wife, Karen (high "C"), waits on me as well—she waits on me to use my *own* hands and feet to get what I want! She got that from *her* mother. I remember sitting at Karen's house when we were dating, watching TV and saying to Karen (in the presence of her mother), "Hey, how about getting me something to drink?" Karen's mom looked at me and she walked over, grabbed me by the arm, and gave me a tour of the pantry and refrigerator so I would know where to find things for myself.

After I grew up and went away to college, my mom went back to work. The people she worked with and for at City Hall appreciated her steadfastness and her ability to work hard at her job. When she passed away in 1984, there were hundreds of people at her funeral who commented to me about how much they appreciated her sensitive and genuine spirit.

### HOW GOD MODELS THE "S" STYLE

No passage of Scripture pictures God as a supportive parent better than Psalm 23. This familiar psalm expresses the calm and peaceful relationship that God leads us into:

The LORD is my shepherd, I shall not be in want.
He makes me lie down in green pastures,
  he leads me beside quiet waters,
  he restores my soul.
He guides me in paths of righteousness
  for his name's sake.
Even though I walk
  through the valley of the shadow of death,
I will fear no evil,
  for you are with me;
  your rod and your staff,
  they comfort me.
You prepare a table before me in the presence of my enemies.
You anoint my head with oil;

my cup overflows.
Surely goodness and love will follow me
all the days of my life,
and I will dwell in the house of the LORD
forever.

In other Scripture, God is described as our helper (Psalm 33:20; 46:1; 121:1; 124:8; Isaiah 41:10; Hebrews 13:6), redeemer (Psalm 103:3), comforter (2 Corinthians 1:3-4), and friend (John 15:13-15). All of these illustrate our God's steady, devoted, caring nature.

In response to our heavenly Father's supportive parenting style, we can follow Lamentation 3:22-26 and place our hope solidly in His care:

Because of the LORD's great love we are not consumed,
for his compassions never fail.
They are new every morning;
great is your faithfulness.
I say to myself, "The LORD is my portion;
therefore, I will wait for him."
The LORD is good to those whose hope is in him,
to the one who seeks him;
it is good to wait quietly
for the salvation of the LORD.

### THE DANGER OF ACCOMMODATION

A common weakness of "S" individuals is that they become overly accommodating. They can become so concerned that others are happy, and so fearful of losing a close relationship, that they allow others to walk all over them.

**Supportive** —*Fear of losing the security of a close relationship.*→ **Accommodating**

A friend told me about a married couple he counseled. The wife was seeing another man, and the husband knew about it. "I don't like it," he said. "But I want her to be happy."

The counselor was amazed. How could this man actually sit back and watch his wife date another man? The counselor then looked up the man's DISC profile and found him to be an extremely high "S."

"Your desire is to please people," he told the husband, "but this is going way too far. If you really love your wife, you will not tolerate her dating another person." It turned out that this kind of overly accommodating behavior had caused his wife to conclude that he didn't care about their marriage.

While that story may be a bit extreme, it does illustrate the danger of accommodation. Supportive parents sometimes go so far to meet their children's needs that they may actually stunt their maturity and leave them unprepared to face life on their own.

In their excellent book, *Parenting with Love and Logic*, Foster Cline and Jim Fay call this style the "Helicopter Parent":

> Some parents think love means rotating their lives around their children. They are helicopter parents. They hover over and rescue their children whenever trouble arises. They're forever running lunches and permission slips and homework assignments to school; they're always pulling their children out of jams; not a day goes by when they're not protecting little junior from something—usually from a learning experience the child needs or deserves. As soon as their children send up an SOS flare, helicopter parents, who are hovering nearby, swoop in and shield the children from teachers, playmates, and other demands that appear hostile.[3]

The authors go on to say that, while these "loving" parents may feel they are easing their children's paths into adulthood, they actually are setting them up for years of struggle. Having been sheltered all their lives, children of helicopter parents are unprepared and unequipped for the challenges of life.

I know one helicopter mother who won't let her children play with the kids in the neighborhood, fearing they might catch a cold. While protecting her son and daughter from germs, she is stunting their emotional and social development.

Another common problem of accommodating parents is that they tend to easily *give in* to avoid arguments. They want to keep the peace at all costs.

*Child:* "Mom, can I get these red shoes?"

*Mom:* "No, Chelsea. We talked about this earlier. You need white shoes to wear with your Easter dress and a black pair to wear with your school uniform. We can only get one pair today, white or black."

*Child* (loudly and with emotion): "I want the red ones!"

*Mom:* "No, we just don't have the money for two pair."

*Child:* "I hate you. You never get me what I want."

*Mom:* "That's a terrible thing to say. You know you don't hate me. And besides, you need to talk more quietly. People are beginning to stare."

*Child* (even louder now): "I *do* hate you and I don't care who is listening."

*Mom:* "Okay, okay...calm down. We will get the red shoes just this once. But you have to promise not to ask for anything else."

*Child:* "I promise."

Allowing children to push through limits and boundaries is unwise and unhealthy for them in the long run. Children with accommodating parents can become overly dependent on their parents' help even after they are grown.

One more thing. A high "S" parent who has become accommodating may find it difficult to share her feelings, especially if she feels put upon or used. Since these parents are accustomed to making personal sacrifices to meet the needs of others, they may struggle internally with not feeling appreciated. They often feel they are taken for granted.

Remember, high "S" individuals need you to show sincere, tangible appreciation for all that they do.

### WHAT ACCOMMODATING PARENTS NEED

• As to communication: Be more open with your feelings. Speak up when you are upset about something, rather than internalize your feelings and frustrations. Be more decisive, and stick to the rules you develop.

• As to pace: There are times when you must speed up and push yourself out of your comfort zone. Take more initiative when appropriate.

• As to priorities: Your love and care for your family is unmistakable. However, do not allow yourself to become a rescuer who constantly bails your kids out of trouble. Allow your children to experience the logical consequences of their actions. For your kids to become responsible adults, they must learn how to handle the difficulties they get themselves into. How often you practice this may need to vary according to the age and behavioral style of your children.

• As to change: Learn that change is inevitable. Families move, children grow up and leave home...things simply do not stay the same. Preserve and treasure the past with traditions, collectibles, and memories, but do not fear healthy change.

• As to yourself: It is not unspiritual or unloving to take time for yourself. Plan at least one thing a week that fills your emotional tank, which you so readily empty for others.

## THE SOFT-HEARTED CHILD

One thing you don't usually have to worry about with "S" children is whether or not they have friends. They may not blend in as quickly as the "I" child, but they will be selective and make a few good friends. They tend to be quiet, easygoing, and concerned about pleasing others. They are well-liked by others because they are so willing to accommodate. If you have an "S" child, other parents may tell you, "Your child is such a good friend for mine—and she's so easy to have over!"

Soft-hearted children enjoy being part of a group, and in athletics they make good team players. Since they are slow-paced, they don't attack projects quickly, but instead like to move through them methodically.

They also like to be shown how to do something. Don't ask your "S" child to make some tuna sandwiches and expect her to figure out how to do it herself. Instead, take a few minutes to show her, step by step, how to fix it, and in the future she'll follow that procedure precisely. This is extremely important for teachers to know. Often a high "S" child will do poor work because she does not understand exactly how something is to be done, and she may be too shy or embarrassed to ask.

"S" children respond favorably to a well-established, clearly defined routine. They feel most safe and secure when in familiar surroundings. They fear change from the status quo and strive to keep things as they are. They dislike surprises or disruptions in what they are used to. Constant changes, confusion, and crises cause them a great deal of inner turmoil. These children need to know in advance that a major change is coming.

They are more vulnerable to family instability than other children. They will feel a great deal of stress if you do not display unity in your marriage.

Many parents say their "S" kids are fairly easy to raise. The challenge for adults is to avoid taking advantage of their accommodating nature.

These children tend to get along well with everyone and do well with the more people-oriented parenting styles. At times, they may have some internal struggles if both parents are high "D" or high "C," or if they live in a highly task-oriented home environment. They need to feel relationally close in order to thrive.

My friend Sandra Merwin is a counselor, teacher, and writer in Minneapolis. She is a storehouse of great anecdotes about children who exhibit the different DISC behavioral styles.[4] To illustrate the easygoing nature of a high "S" child, she told me about Jim, who tried out for his high school basketball team. His parents knew he was a good player, so they were shocked when he came home from tryouts and said he hadn't qualified for the team.

When they asked what happened, Jim said the coach had given each candidate one chance to make a basket from the free throw line. Only those who made the shot were on the team, and Jim happened to miss.

The parents were floored. How could a coach determine his players with such a crazy test? Even Michael Jordan might miss his one attempt under those circumstances.

They later learned the coach was actually using the free throw to test each player's desire and competitiveness. The players who pleaded with the coach for another chance were allowed to continue trying out for the team. But Jim, an easygoing kid, just accepted his fate and left the tryout.

It turned out that Jim had his chance for redemption. He made the junior varsity team and was able to show that even easygoing kids can be competitive. Within a few weeks, he was promoted to the varsity squad.

Soft-hearted children dislike change. They don't like to change their schedules, and the thought of moving to another house or city will cause great stress. One girl, who lived in a family of fast-paced "D's" who enjoy change, wrote the following for a school paper: "No one in my family likes to do the same things ever. I like to do the same things all the time. My mom is always busy doing a lot of things. I don't like doing a lot of things. I like doing one or two things. In the evenings we always have to go someplace and do something. When I'm grown up I'm not going to always have to go someplace and do something."

This poor child was feeling crushed in her family. Nobody took the time to understand her needs.

## WORKING WITH AN "S" CHILD

Here are some ways you can help an "S" child reach her full potential:

- Make your home as stable as possible. Reduce the number of quick changes by preparing her in advance. Remember, she needs lots of time to prepare for change. Don't force her to make quick decisions or adapt too quickly.
- Encourage her to express her feelings more often.
- Help her set goals and reward her by expressing your sincere appreciation.
- Provide personal assurances and support.
- Make every effort to keep your promises. If something comes up that prevents you from following through, understand that she may struggle with disappointment. Be apologetic and empathize with her,

rather than insisting that she act reasonably or logically about it.

• Make sure to answer her "how" questions. Expect to give step-by-step explanations.

• Be warm and personal with her before involving her in a task.

• Help her make decisions on her own by starting early to present choices. When she asks you what you would do, say, "I don't know. What do you think?"

• Watch your tone with this child. Loud, angry reactions can cause her to shut down internally.

• Don't be domineering or demanding.

• Don't make decisions for her. Show her how to make decisions on her own.

• Don't force her to agree with you. She will tend to give in to you rather than express her own desires. But she will submerge her feelings, and they will come out later.

## ARE YOU A HIGH "S"?

Below is a list of traits characteristic of the "S" individual. Think about your behaviors and interactions with other people. Highlight those that you feel describe you:

I like to help people when I see they need something.
I'm a good listener, and I'm able to calm people who are upset.
It takes me a while to adjust to change; I prefer things to stay the same.
I'm generally an easygoing person.
If I'm upset, I usually hold my emotions inside.
I like to build solid, lasting friendships.
I'm good at short-term planning.
People see me as patient and uncomplaining.
I usually find ways to avoid conflict and maintain peace.
Fast-paced people get frustrated with me because of my slower pace.
I don't like projects where I'm expected to figure out how something is to be done; show me how to do it, and I'll do it well.
People generally feel relaxed around me.
Sometimes I'm too soft-hearted.
I'll lead if I need to, but generally I'm more of a follower.
I enjoy being part of a team.

I like sincere praise, but I may get embarrassed if too much attention is focused on me.
I'm a dependable worker; I take my job seriously.
I often have a difficult time making quick decisions.

## NOTES

1. Tony Alessandra and Michael O'Conner, *People Smart* (La Jolla, Calif.: Keynote Publishing Company, 1990), 221.

2. Ibid., 221.

3. Foster Cline and Jim Fay, *Parenting with Love and Logic* (Colorado Springs: NavPress, 1990), 23-24.

4. Sandra Merwin's excellent book, *Figuring Kids Out*, can be obtained by writing her in care of TigerLily Press, 4655 Baker Road, Minnetonka, MN 55343.

I value independence [illegible]

CHAPTER SEVEN

# THE "C" STYLE

## CORRECTIVE PARENTS, CONSCIENTIOUS CHILDREN

Of the four primary behavioral styles, the "C" (cautious, conscientious, compliant, correct) may be the most complex. High "C" individuals often are reserved and quiet, yet there is much more going on under the surface than most people realize.

Here are some of the comments I often hear others make about high "C's":

"He's so quiet when you meet him, but when you get below the surface you find he's really interesting."

"She never says much during class discussions, but in her written papers I can tell that she has a better grasp of the issues than those who talk all the time."

"I didn't realize she was so creative."

"He often appears so unemotional to me, so I was really surprised the other day when I saw how affectionate he was with his wife and daughters."

"He'll sit through a two-hour meeting and listen to everyone else express their opinions about a problem we're facing, and when he finally speaks up at the end, he usually gives us the best solution."

"Sometimes I don't think she likes me, but then at other times she's so warm and friendly. It's hard to figure her out."

Because they are more reserved by nature, always remember that the phrase, "What you see is what you get" definitely does not apply to high "C's." First impressions are rarely sufficient for you to know this style.

High "C's" are highly task-oriented, capable, competent, and quality-conscious. They tend to be private people who feel comfortable being alone and working independently.

Their independence comes from an emphasis on internal thinking strengths—looking to resources within rather than without. This bent gives the impression to others of quiet self-confidence, self-reliance, self-discipline, and self-directedness.

Being more emotionally contained, they hold their feelings in rather than express them. They tend to be somewhat cautious in establishing new relationships and usually wait for the other person to take the initiative.

### SEVEN PROMINENT CHARACTERISTICS OF THE CORRECTIVE/CONSCIENTIOUS STYLE

• Maintains high standards: They measure themselves and their behavior along a strict yardstick of a strong, demanding inner authority. Whatever they put their signature on, they want to reflect excellence. When they don't meet their inner standards, they often feel guilt and anxiety. They may even struggle with low self-esteem because they don't come up to those personal standards of excellence. They fear criticism of their work and will work hard to avoid it at all costs.

• Attentive to key details: High "C" individuals pay close attention to important details and want you to do so as well. They like their tasks and projects to be complete to the final detail, without mistakes or flaws. Because they are so detail conscious, they are seldom wrong.

• Self-disciplined: They take their work seriously and are capable of intense, single-minded effort. They regard self-discipline as essential to success and acceptable performance.

• Cautious: Careful, calculating, and prudent in all areas of their lives, they tend to avoid risks and are not given to reckless abandon or wild excess. They tend not to do anything without the assurance of high-quality success. They do not express their feelings easily or comfortably. As a result, others may perceive them to be aloof and reserved.

• Analytical: They are ruled by their heads. They examine situations and think through their plans before taking action. They concentrate more on thought than action, and facts more than feelings. Highly objective, they rarely let emotions, whims, or impulsive reactions get the best of them.

• Highly intuitive: Because they are constantly collecting and processing data, high "C's" are able to accurately read people and situations with a logic-based, inner intuition.

• Does things the "right way": With their analytical bent, these individuals come to a conclusion about the "correct" way to perform different procedures. They are confident their ways are the best, whether they involve organizing a multi-million-dollar investment portfolio or loading a dishwasher. They easily discern right and wrong, but tend to have difficulty deciding between two "good" or "right" things.

High "C's" can be cautious about extending friendship. Initially, they may be more concerned with maintaining the quality of the work to be done than the relational aspects of the job. People and friendships may be very important to "C's," though this may not seem to be the case at first.

Since they are reserved around people, high "C's" need a lot of prodding before they will speak or perform in public. Their natural style discourages them from taking bold leadership. This doesn't mean they can't; it simply means that showing leadership takes more of their energy because they are pushing themselves out of their comfort zones.

They are slower in making decisions because they want to make the "right" decision. They will move with caution and deliberation, gathering all the facts, being highly concerned about the minutest details and all possibilities. However, once the decision is made it will be lasting.

One interesting characteristic of many high "C's" is that they sometimes find it difficult to fall asleep. They need to make a special effort to turn off their mental processing an hour before bedtime so that they don't lie in bed analyzing the many things running through their minds.

A high "C" friend told me about the night she fell exhausted into bed after a particularly busy day. Her husband asked, "What are you doing tomorrow?" and she replied, "Is this something you need to know, or are you just making conversation? I don't want to start thinking about tomorrow if I don't have to."

The husband said, "Oh, I was just talking. I don't need to know." But by then it was too late. Her mind was in gear again and she had trouble falling asleep.

The greatest strengths of high "C's" are their accuracy, dependability, independence, follow through, and organization. Their greatest weaknesses are their tendencies to be picky, critical, and overly cautious.

One lady said that her high "C" husband spent one year before deciding on a pair of dress shoes. She was concerned because he was now interested in buying a new car. "If the shoes took a year," she said, "then I figure our new car will be in our garage by the next time Haley's comet comes around!"

### A Biblical Example

When God wanted to put His law in stone, He looked to a high "C" person, Moses, to accurately record and proclaim it to the nation of Israel. When you consider the detailed historical account recorded in the first five books of the Bible, as well as the multitude of laws (just read through Leviticus for a refresher), it becomes clear that someone with an analytical and organized mind was needed to painstakingly record and preserve the laws of God.

The way God got Moses' attention was different from the way He dealt with Paul. On the Damascus road, God used direct confrontation, knocking Paul to his knees with a blinding light. With Moses, God used a light—a small one, flickering on a mountainside. In characteristic high "C" fashion, Moses' curiosity was aroused, and he went to investigate.

In Exodus 3, God explains in detail—just what a "C" would want—His plans for the enslaved Jews. He told Moses why He was taking action (v. 7), He gave Moses a description of His plan (v. 8), and He told Moses the part he would play in the plan (v. 10). God spelled out the specific details as to who, what, why, and how He would deliver His people.

Moses asked many questions about the task God wanted him to undertake, and God patiently answered each one. But Moses needed special reassurance that everything would go as planned. Exodus 4 tells how God used three illustrations to verify His message to Moses:

- He turned a staff into a serpent.
- He turned Moses' healthy hand into a leprous one and then healed it.
- He turned water from the Nile into blood.

Moses was running out of excuses, but he didn't want to confront Pharaoh alone. So Moses—again in high "C" fashion—offered another reason he was not the man for the job: He was not a good public speaker! God began to lose patience, but He allowed Moses to take along his brother Aaron to be his voice.

Based on the story of Moses and the stories of biblical characters I've told in the previous three chapters, we can see how God dealt with each person in different ways. His methods seem to coincide with the motivations and needs of each person's behavioral style. This pattern coincides with how He directs each of us.

### THE CORRECTIVE PARENT

Corrective parents see their primary responsibility as making sure their children turn out right. They try to teach their kids the importance of doing their best and striving for excellence, qualities which are indeed admirable. They want their children to reach their fullest potential and be competent at whatever they choose to do.

"C" parents encourage their children to investigate, study, and ask questions about anything that interests them. They enjoy discussing things on a deeper, more analytical level with their kids. They like to explain their reasons behind making decisions and encourage their children to think before they act.

They tend to be good listeners when their children or spouse are providing information that can be used in the decision-making process.

Usually they anger slowly, and they can be very effective parents in a peaceful environment. Because of their need to explain things, they tend to use a lecture style of parenting and may give more details than some styles ("D's" and "I's") care to hear.

They may come across as unemotional and distant because of their more reserved nature. They are private people and do not readily express their innermost thoughts about a situation.

My wife, Karen, is a high "C/S." She is much more cautious than I am, and that provides a good balance in our home. When we are going on vacation, she makes a long list of everything we need. She begins the packing process by going to Wal-Mart to purchase travel-size necessities. Every suitcase and bag we will take is open and lined up along our bedroom wall. I sometimes call her the family "pilot" because she piles each family member's clothes in stacks on the bed and then transfers the clothes to the suitcases.

In planning a trip, she constantly processes everything that's needed to make it successful—where we will be staying, what clothes we will need for each event we may attend while away, medicines for just in case. She actually seems to enjoy organizing everything into a workable plan. Sometimes I feel that we pack too much, but she rarely leaves anything we need behind.

Even our kids understand her style. Chad's teacher once asked him to tell her about his family and about himself. The first thing he said was, "Well, my mom's a planner. She thinks through everything she does. I'm not a planner. I just take things as they come."

Over the years, I have come to appreciate and value Karen's more cautious nature. Once I was going to buy a used car. I wanted a Honda Prelude, and I found a beauty with low mileage. When I got home and told Karen, she said, "Great. I'm glad you found what you want. The only thing I would like to see you do is take it to a dealership and have them check it out. What if it has been wrecked?"

I wanted that car and really didn't want to fool around with all that hassle, so I said, "Well, the salesman at Big Al's Used Car Emporium assured me that the car had not been wrecked. And besides, I've looked it over and everything checks out."

She said, "I didn't say I didn't want you to have the car. I would just feel better about it if you would have it checked out." I finally agreed and took it to the dealership. To make a long story shorter, the car had been wrecked. The mechanic in the body shop showed me how great care had been taken to hide all signs of the accident.

He put it this way, "Mr. Boyd, I know you like this car. But I wouldn't buy this car for my daughter. I don't think it's safe and you won't be able to keep tires on the front end."

I have no doubts; God knew we needed Karen's cautious, conscientious nature as the safeguard in our family.

Corrective style parents do not like conflict and confrontation. They try to correct behavior by logic and reasoning. They prefer discipline like "time outs" and "restrictions" that encourages their children to think about what they've done.

Corrective parents understand that love must have limits, and they tend to focus more on the limit side of things.

### HOW GOD MODELS THE "C" STYLE

Though God is a God of mercy and compassion, He also corrects and disciplines His children when they live their lives independently from Him. His correction is always from a heart of love because He knows and wants what is ultimately best for us: to walk in His ways and follow His truth. Hebrews 12:6-11 puts it this way:

> "The Lord disciplines those he loves, and he punishes everyone he accepts as a son." Endure hardship as discipline; God is treating you as sons. For what son is not disciplined by his father? If you are not disciplined (and everyone undergoes discipline), then you are illegitimate children and not true sons. Moreover, we have all had human fathers who disciplined us and we respected them for it. How much more should we submit to the Father of our spirits and live! Our fathers disciplined us for a little while as they thought best; but God disciplines us for our good, that we may share in his holiness. No discipline seems pleasant at the time, but painful. Later on, however, it produces a harvest of righteousness and peace for those who have been trained by it.

Our response to our heavenly Father's corrective parenting style needs to be one of confessing where we are wrong or where we may have behaved unwisely. He also desires that we be open and teachable to the truths of His Word.

In 2 Timothy 3:16-17, we are told: "All Scripture is God-breathed and is useful for teaching, rebuking, correcting and training in righteousness, so that the man of God may be thoroughly equipped for every good work." The Bible teaches—shows us the right way to live in relation to God and others; reproves—points out where we get off track or out of line with His truth; corrects—tells us exactly how to get back on the right track; and trains us in right living—shows us how to avoid making the same mistake again and leads us further into wise living. Our Father couldn't have given us a more helpful, thorough Book!

### INEFFECTIVE "C" PARENTS

When "C"-style parents allow their fear of making mistakes to govern their actions, they may become overly perfectionistic.

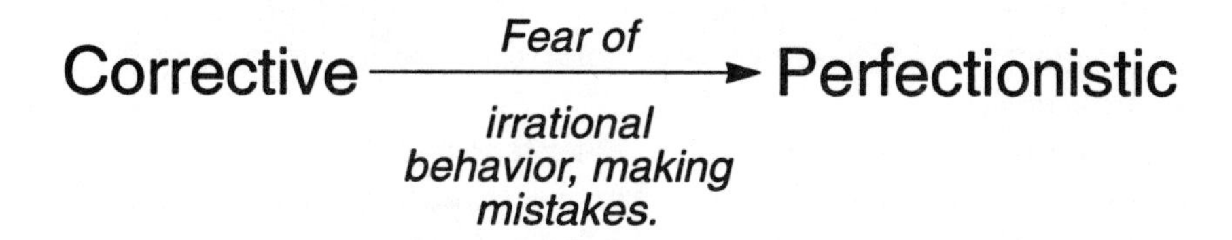


Perfectionistic parents want things done the "right" way and will not tolerate any deviation from that. They try to maintain control by getting their children to comply to their high standards.

They tend to be performance-based in their approach to parenting because they have such high standards. To them a good parent is the parent whose children conform to a certain prescribed blueprint.

They tend to be serious-minded, controlled, methodical, and rule-oriented. They may find it hard to click with their child on an emotional level. They may be afraid of closeness in general and find themselves shying away from closeness with their child.

One perfectionistic mother told me that she didn't feel her kids needed to be told she loved them. "I don't need to tell my children I love them. They should know I do because of what I do for them."

These parents fear making mistakes and, worst of all, appearing to be a "bad" parent. Like the autocratic parent, the perfectionistic parent may also find it hard to admit when he is wrong.

Because of his desire to go by the book, even when a child does something the "right" way, the perfectionistic parent will find something that can be improved upon next time. The child hears, "You did a good job, *but...*"

Long term, this feeling of never measuring up can damage a child's self-esteem. He may give up and think, "There's no use trying. I'll never be able to do it well enough anyway."

The perfectionistic parent's approach is clear: Do it the right way or not at all.

## WHAT PERFECTIONISTIC PARENTS NEED

To strengthen their parenting skills, Corrective parents need to apply some of the strengths of the Interactive- and Supportive-style parents. They will help avoid becoming perfectionistic by having more fun with their kids, remembering to see their kids as people rather than concentrating only on performance, and by not taking everything so seriously.

• As to being right: Accept the fact that no one is right all the time. That's okay. Unhealthy perfectionism can cause children to feel that their attempts to please you will never be good enough. It is okay to make a mistake every once in a while. And if you have a child who likes to experiment with different ways of doing things, allow that creativity to express itself.

• As to conflict: Face conflict, rather than avoid it.

• As to communication: There are several things to keep in mind here: 1) Open up and verbalize your feelings more. Do not expect family members to be able to read your mind. 2) Guard against over analyzing and then over explaining things to others. Not everyone needs or enjoys the same level of detail and thinking that you do. 3) Also, be careful with questions. At times, too many questions can come across as interrogation rather than conversation. 4) Voice your disapproval or criticism in caring ways.

• As to priority: Be careful that necessary tasks, chores, and projects do not become more important than your children. Spending the day according to plan is important, but plans must not take precedence over your relationship with your children. As a high "I" would say, "Lighten up!" Don't take everything so seriously.

• As to pace: Relax and become more spontaneous in dealing with other family members.

• As to your strength of analysis: Sometimes you can become so concerned with the trees that you fail to see the forest. Beware of getting bogged down in the "paralysis of analysis."

A high "C" mother recently told me that she always battles her tendency toward being overly corrective and perfectionistic. "I was never more aware of it than when I was trying to teach my daughter to cook," she said. "Allison, is a high 'I' and she loves to cook. But she doesn't want to follow the recipe. She wants to take a more creative approach and experiment with recipes. I have a hard time not stepping in and saying, 'Do it this way.' "

## THE CONSCIENTIOUS CHILD

"C" kids are analytical thinkers. They are serious about life. Whatever they do, they want it to reflect their high standards.

Their sense of organization starts early. They stack their toys, line them up, work puzzles, and do projects with precision. They generally have a place for everything and have everything in its place.

I walked into Kristi's closet the other day to hang up some clothes that had just been ironed. As I entered, I noticed that each one of her built-in bookshelves housed a certain kind of toy: dolls on one, stuffed animals on another, glass and porcelain figurines on another. Each cubicle was perfectly arranged.

Kristi loves to keep everything in her room neat and orderly. She will lift her furniture and put the things on the floor on her bed so her mother or I can vacuum underneath.

"C" kids tend to be perfectionists and don't do anything without a pretty good chance of success. When Kristi was learning to write, her teacher gave the class an assignment to write a letter to the soldiers during the Gulf War. First, Kristi dictated what she wanted to say. Then I wrote it out for her on a sheet of paper so she could write hers "right." (These were her instructions, not mine.) Then she went, letter by letter, crossing off my letters as she copied them down in her own handwriting. She worked cautiously until she had completed the whole thing.

High "C" children may struggle with self-esteem issues if they fail to meet their own high standards. Their goal is to be correct. They tend to prefer to do things by themselves. That way, they can ensure things are done according to their standards.

Sometimes their orientation to detail may come out in their art. One mother described her daughter by saying, "I noticed when she was young and would draw a picture of a house, if there were four steps on the front, there would be four steps in our picture. If there's a hinge missing on a window, it'll be that way in the picture."

These kids are very observant, taking in all that is going on around them, and processing and evaluating what they are experiencing. They may have a sensitive, artistic, or musical nature. They tend to have a surprising store of information. This "know-ability" can make them intolerant of adults who aren't in the know. They may talk early and learn to read earlier than most. They usually enjoy reading books or being read to longer than many other children.

They may express intolerance for people who are not logical and factual. They also may be overeager to help other children learn the "right way" to do things. I heard the story of a kindergartner who noticed that some of his classmates didn't put their treats on a napkin during snack time. He corrected one of them, and his teacher praised him. So for the next few weeks he took it upon himself to act as the snack monitor. When the teacher had a conference with his parents, she mentioned, "I would somehow like to help Josh not be the teacher during snack time!"

High "C" kids tend to avoid interpersonal aggression. They often will agree, rather than fight about things. They quickly learn how to get along with others by finding out what is expected and trying hard to meet those expectations. They tend to appear to be undemanding and don't always share how they feel. Their demands can come out in a somewhat indirect (rather than straightforward) fashion.

They tend to be very introspective. One high "I" mother came up to me in tears after a Child's Design workshop. She said, "I finally understand my daughter. She's a high 'C,' but it bothers me that she seems so sad and serious. The other day, she came home from school and said, 'I feel like I'm the only one in the whole school who is like me.' It broke my heart. I want her to be happy. What can I do?"

I told this mother the first thing she needed to do was let her daughter be a "C." She needed to let the girl know that it's okay to be concerned about things and then slowly draw her out. She also should be careful to talk about how her daughter feels at times when her daughter wants to talk, and not pressure her to talk when she wants privacy.

I also explained that if she made a big deal over worrying, her daughter would worry about worrying. She would get into a loop of worrying about worrying about worrying that would take her deeper into her introspection.

Conscientious children want others to view them as being competent and capable. Because they want to do the "right" thing, they have a tendency to be too analytical. Often, an adult of a different style will say, "You know what your problem is? You think too much!"

With their strong internal environment, it may be hard for "C" kids to take criticism, especially if they think it's unfair. In one case, a little girl was riding her bike home from school, and some road construction prevented her from following the route her mother wanted her to take. This mother was outside when the daughter returned home and scolded her for disobeying the rules.

The daughter burst into tears and, typical of high "C's," she couldn't explain her emotions right away, so she ran off crying. Once she had a chance to bring her emotions into harmony, she was able to explain to her mother what had happened.

High "C" children want reasons for the things they are expected to do. Their "why" questions can become annoying to some parents. They have curious minds, so they need opportunities to experiment, find out, and get answers to their "what if" and "what would happen if" questions.

## WORKING WITH A "C" CHILD

• Carefully bring him out of his shell with, "What are you thinking or feeling?" kinds of questions. However, be careful with your timing and do not invade his privacy.

• Allow him time to do quality work. Don't push or rush him. When he procrastinates, it's because he wants to do the job "right."

• Help him develop a tolerance for imperfection.

• Focus on who he is, not just what he does. Affirm his high value as a person despite what he does.

• Keep your promises and follow through on key details.

• Approach him in a direct, straightforward way. Stick to the subject.

• If you disagree with him, clearly explain why. Always answer his "why" questions. Allow time for his questions and give in-depth explanations.

• Allow him time alone to recharge. He needs time to "percolate" and think. Also allow him time to be disappointed when he doesn't meet his own high expectations before trying to encourage him.

• Support his thoughtful, analytical approach to things. He never acts or talks without a lot of thought.

• Show appreciation for the quality of his work. Be very specific in your praise. He may not feel encouraged by broad compliments such as "Great job!" "Wow, this is terrific!" or "Your solo was outstanding!" Describe *what* was good: "I can see you worked very hard to get that solo note perfect."

• Don't tell him his concerns, questions, or problems are stupid or unimportant.

• Don't rush him with decision-making.

• Don't be vague about what is expected of either of you.

• Don't threaten or confront in loud, angry tones. He will withdraw and may appear to comply under great force, but deep inside he is planning his next move.

• Don't offer him gimmicky incentives to get him to do something. He can see right through manipulation.

• Don't be overly emotional when trying to convince. Stick to facts and reliable sources.

• Allow him time to think before you expect a response.

• Avoid interrupting him when he is working.

• Give him rituals to follow.

• Before you expect him to go to sleep, allow him time to "turn off his brain." For some, reading will help. You may need to help him think through the day. Help him examine failures and successes and make decisions, so that he doesn't lie awake thinking about them.

• Be careful not to set standards that are too high. His own personal standards are already high enough that you shouldn't weigh him down too much with yours.

## ARE YOU A HIGH "C"?

Below is a list of traits characteristic of the "C"-style individual. Think about your behavior and interactions with other people. Highlight those statements that you feel describe you.

I like to focus on doing things right.
I'm good at organizing my affairs.
Accuracy is important to me.
I have a strong respect for rules and authority.
I have high standards for myself—sometimes too high.
People see me as formal, reserved, and serious.
Sometimes I'm hard to please.
I need all the facts and information I can gather before making a decision.
I don't like to make mistakes.
I'm a good planner; I'm able to break down big projects into small parts.
I analyze things thoroughly in my mind.
Under pressure, I tend to avoid confrontation.
Some people see me as slow; I prefer to use the word "methodical."
I hold my emotions inside and only let them out in situations where I feel comfortable.
Generally I'm tactful, diplomatic, and courteous.

CHAPTER EIGHT

# BECOMING A STUDENT OF YOUR CHILD

There is a danger in reading a book like this. Really, it's the same danger inherent in all parenting books.

In my library I have no less than fifty books on the subject of child-rearing. Like you, I want the best for my children, and I try to take advantage of books and tapes and seminars to help me learn more. The danger comes when I become a student of parenting techniques rather than a student of my children.

More than anything else, the message of this book is that you need to study your child. The DISC model simply gives you a language to discover and discuss your child's behavior style, so that you can value and appreciate that style rather than see it as a threat or a deficiency.

After reading the last four chapters, you probably have a good idea of what your own primary behavioral style is. Hopefully you're also beginning to formulate some ideas about whether your child is "D" (Determined), "I" (Influencing), "S" (Soft-hearted), or "C" (Conscientious).

Some parents have no trouble determining which primary behavioral style describes their children. You hear them make statements like these:

"She has never given us one bit of trouble. She was such an easy baby."

"He has never been able to sit still. He jumps into everything with both feet—including mud puddles!"

"From day one, I just knew this child would become a lawyer. He argues about anything and everything."

"Our two children are exact opposites. One sits for hours, alone in her room, playing with her dolls. The other child thinks being alone is punishment."

But this doesn't mean that a person's behavior style will necessarily be obvious from birth. Many of you may not be able to discern it until the child is six or eight years old—or even older.

There are several reasons why you may have difficulty determining your child's behavioral style:

*Your child is "in process."* As she moves through various stages of development, she experiments with different behaviors to see how they fit. She wants to know if what she does squares with how she thinks and feels. As a result, she repeats comfortable behaviors and avoids those that cause problems or don't feel natural. In this way, she develops patterns of behavior according to what works and what doesn't. This can cause confusion for parents who are trying to figure out their child!

*As your child grows older, you increasingly see her in restricted circumstances.* As she grows up, she will spend more and more time away from you with friends and at school. In these different environments, she may behave differently. She may feel the need to adapt her behavioral style to meet the needs of different situations, or it may just be that different aspects of her style are surfacing with different groups of people.

As an only child, I grew up, for the most part, as an easygoing and compliant boy at home. In high school, however, I played in a rock band and was the class clown. I acted out whole comedy routines in front of the class. When we had a substitute teacher, I pretended to be an exchange student from Spain.

When reports began to trickle home from teachers about my behavior, my parents couldn't believe them. "Who? Our son did that?" Obviously, my "at home" style was different from my "at school" style. When I was at home I adapted my behavior to be obedient to my parents.

*You may be too close to your child to see her objectively.* You may not yet be aware of how your behavioral style affects your judgment. You may overlook whole parts of her personality because your hopes, dreams, and fears for her color your perception.

*Your child is a complex combination of several behavioral styles.* She is a blend of all four DISC styles in varying intensities. Most people have a primary DISC style, but usually they score high in one or sometimes two other categories as well. So avoid putting your child into one category only.[1]

This happened with my son, Chad. We knew that he was a high "D" child, but for quite awhile we missed the fact that he also scored high in the "I" category. Karen and I are task-oriented, so perhaps we were reading our own behavior into Chad more than we should have.

Then we began to notice a whole side of Chad that we had been blind to. He could walk up to a group of boys he didn't know, jump in, and start talking. We realized that his tendency to interrupt us and ask about other subjects while we were helping him with homework wasn't always an attempt to control us, but was sometimes an honest desire to talk. To say the least, it radically altered our perception of Chad.

So what am I saying? Don't lock your child into certain ways of being and conclude that you have everything figured out. The purpose of this information is to provide you with a tool that can assist you in discovering and encouraging your child's unique strengths as she matures. Our goal is to help you help your child to discover her life "style" so that when she is older, she will stay true to course.

### STEPS TO STUDYING YOUR CHILD

As you begin your study course, here are some suggestions:

1. *Observe your child in as many different situations as possible.* Look for patterns of behavior. Watch your child at play on the playground at school or in the park. How does she interact with other children and with adults? How does she act when she meets new people? What does she like to do to relax? What interests her? What types of projects does she enjoy? What type of imagination does she display?

When you watch your child, don't look for behaviors you can direct and correct. Just observe her. If you are a task-oriented parent ("D" or "C"), this will be a challenge!

2. *Solicit the opinions of other people who see your child in different situations.* Talk to her friend's mother and father and to her teachers. Ask friends and members of your extended family what types of behavior they observe in your child. Also, be sure to listen with an open mind. If you want to be a student of your child, you'll have to accept the possibility that she may not fit your previous picture of her at all.

3. *Take your best guess.* From the information you gather, form a hypothesis. Then watch and wait. Is the behavior you usually see consistent with what you know about her DISC style(s)? What is the same? What is different? How does your child's teacher see her? Have the teacher complete a copy of "The Child Behavioral Style Inventory," found at the end of this chapter, and compare your perceptions. How are your perceptions alike? How are they different?

4. *Watch for secondary patterns.* Read through all the behavioral style descriptions to see what matches your child. Chances are you'll find she will have a dominant or core style and a secondary one.

5. *Be open to modifying your perceptions of your child.* One thing is certain: your child is changing and growing. Let her become—don't try to make her *be.* Never try to mold your child to fit a certain style. Use the

DISC model to understand and appreciate how God has made people different. Use it to affirm and encourage growth according to your child's bent, but be careful not to lock her into a certain way of being.

6. *Listen to your spouse.* It is not uncommon for two parents to see the same child differently. Why? Because their interactions with that child may be completely different.

One corporate vice-president scored his son as a "D" and his wife saw the boy as an "S." The father's interaction with the boy was limited to evenings and weekends, when tasks had to be accomplished. Their relationship was goal-oriented—there were things to do and places to go—so he saw his son in that light. His wife, a stay-at-home mom, related to her son on a much more personal level. She saw him as more cooperative and easygoing. Their conclusion was that their son was a combination of both styles.

7. *Use an inventory like the one at the end of this chapter.* Many parents have found "The Child Behavioral Style Inventory" a good tool in learning about their children. I also recommend that you obtain a *Child Discovery Profile* or a *Teen Discovery Profile* (see Appendix C) in order to see how your child sees herself. Using profiles and inventories help you begin forming a hypothesis about what your child's style may be.

Once you have an idea about your child's behavioral style, how do you apply this knowledge to parenting?

Good question. The answer? Do it very, very carefully.

Psalm 127:3 states that "sons are a heritage from the LORD, children a reward from him." Each gift has been designed by God Himself as a unique creation. Once you understand this unique design, you can work within that framework to train your child up "in the way he should go." By doing so, you become partners with God in maximizing your child's God-given potential.

In the next few chapters, I'll show you how.

***Note: As you fill out the following inventory, keep a couple of things in mind:***

*1. The DISC information describes behavioral tendencies. It is deliberately designed as a practical generalization of how people tend to behave. It is not intended to give a complete picture of one's personality, or to lock people into hard and fast categories.*

*2. Behavioral scientists tell us that people are motivated by two basic drives. Our personal energies flow from our needs-drives and our values-drives. This survey focuses only on "needs-driven behavior."*

## THE CHILD BEHAVIORAL STYLE INVENTORY

Write your child's name here: ______________________________

As you think about your child, rank from most (4) to least (1) the characteristics and behaviors which describe how you see your child in each group of four traits listed below. (To be consistent with our approach in this book, we have used feminine pronouns—"she," "her"—throughout this inventory. Substitute "he" and "him" if appropriate.)

### 1

a.___ This child is very strong-willed and stubborn. She is determined to get what she wants when she wants it.

b.___ This child never slows down. She wants to have fun, even when playtime is over and it's time to settle down.

c.___ This child is generally in a positive mood. She smiles and laughs more than she cries.

d.___ This child's first contact with strangers usually causes her to turn away or cling to her parent. She is slow to accept new people. She withdraws at first and adapts very slowly.

### 2

a.___ This child acts quickly and independently and likes to do things herself.

b.___ This child displays intense emotional highs and lows. She acts out her feelings and has a flair for the dramatic.

c.___ This child is generally seen as calm and easygoing. Her intensity of reactions is low or mild.

d.___ This child likes privacy and may at times appear to be a loner or unsociable.

### 3

a.___ This child is generally not overly responsive to affection.

b.___ This child is generally optimistic and enthusiastic in most situations.

c.___ This child is less active toward trying new things and usually prefers the old and familiar.

d.___ This child asks lots of questions and prefers to take her time to think things through before deciding.

### 4

a.___ This child is generally very active. She is an explorer and a risk-taker.

b.___ This child meets people easily and likes to be with people.

c.___ This child cooperates with others and usually gets along with others.

d.___ This child generally takes a cautious, hesitant approach to new situations.

### 5

a.___ This child is hard to lead and more selective about who she follows.

b.___ This child moves from one activity to another, often without finishing.

c.___ This child easily gives in when pressured and may copy the behaviors, rules, and mannerisms of others to the point of exaggeration.

d.___ This child's level of physical activity usually appears to be low or moderate.

### 6

a.___ This child is easily angered and uses force to get what she wants.

b.___ This child may be disorganized, messy, and/or forgetful when it comes to tasks.

c.___ This child has difficulty accepting sudden changes. She can be stubborn about wanting things to stay the same. She wants things to remain calm and peaceful.

d.___ This child's moods generally appear to be mild so that her initial reaction to unfavorable circumstances is quiet and controlled. Her internal reactions may be much stronger.

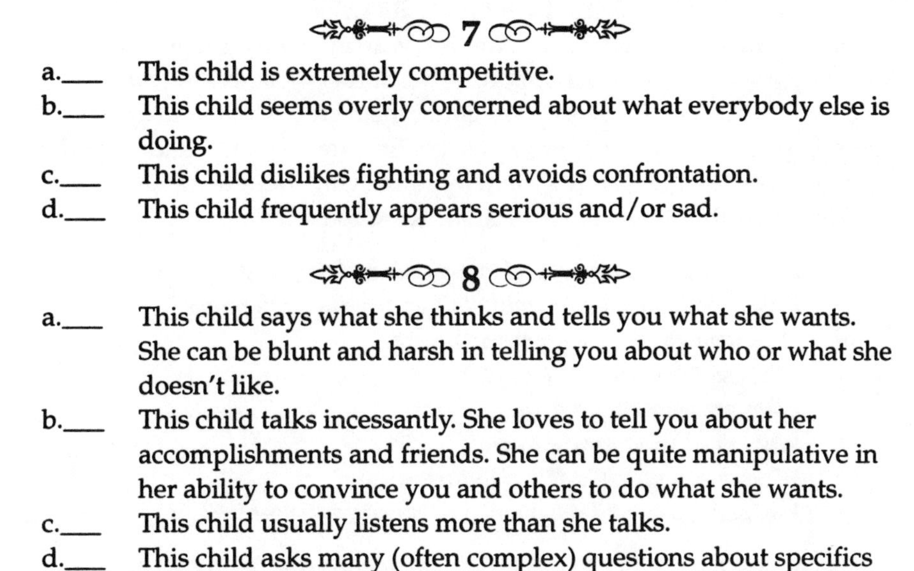

**7**

a.___ This child is extremely competitive.
b.___ This child seems overly concerned about what everybody else is doing.
c.___ This child dislikes fighting and avoids confrontation.
d.___ This child frequently appears serious and/or sad.

**8**

a.___ This child says what she thinks and tells you what she wants. She can be blunt and harsh in telling you about who or what she doesn't like.
b.___ This child talks incessantly. She loves to tell you about her accomplishments and friends. She can be quite manipulative in her ability to convince you and others to do what she wants.
c.___ This child usually listens more than she talks.
d.___ This child asks many (often complex) questions about specifics and needs many detailed explanations.

### TALLY BOX

Transfer your scores from each of the eight groups of traits to the tally box below. Now total the marks in each column. The column with the highest score reflects the predominant behavioral style of your child.

| | | | |
|---|---|---|---|
| 1.a. ____ | 1.b. ____ | 1.c. ____ | 1.d. ____ |
| 2.a. ____ | 2.b. ____ | 2.c. ____ | 2.d. ____ |
| 3.a. ____ | 3.b. ____ | 3.c. ____ | 3.d. ____ |
| 4.a. ____ | 4.b. ____ | 4.c. ____ | 4.d. ____ |
| 5.a. ____ | 5.b. ____ | 5.c. ____ | 5.d. ____ |
| 6.a. ____ | 6.b. ____ | 6.c. ____ | 6.d. ____ |
| 7.a. ____ | 7.b. ____ | 7.c. ____ | 7.d. ____ |
| 8.a. ____ | 8.b. ____ | 8.c. ____ | 8.d. ____ |

Total a. _____ b. _____ c. _____ d. _____

(a. = D; b. = I; c. = S; d. = C)

## FOR FURTHER STUDY

Becoming a student of your children is an everyday assignment. Each day presents countless opportunities and experiences to learn about your children. By closely watching them and listening to them, you will pick up on those hints and signs that are critical to understanding who they are and training them up in the way they should go.

Here are other important questions to be considering:

- *Is your child's activity level fast-paced or slow-paced?*
- *Is your child focused on doing things or being with people?*
- *Does your child most often tell or ask?*
- *What really motivates your child?*
- *What are your child's greatest fears?*
- *What most frustrates your child?*
- *What does your child talk about repeatedly?*
- *What activities and behaviors consistently reappear?*

Becoming a student of your child also means discussing what you see with your children. Make it a practice to ask open-ended questions each day, such as:

- What was the most exciting thing about ______ (e.g., building the tree house, having a friend over)?
- What frustrated you most today when ______ (e.g., Lauren kept taking your toys and telling you what to do)?
- What was the happiest thing that happened today at school? What was the saddest thing that happened?
- What do you like best about ______? What is your favorite ______?

Questions like these not only help you better understand what your child is thinking, feeling, and doing, but over time they will help you see consistent patterns as well.

## NOTE

1. The *Child Discovery Profile* and *The Child's Library of Classical Patterns* mentioned in Appendix C will help you gain in-depth information on your child's unique blend of the DISC styles.

PART III

# BUILDING

CHAPTER NINE

# FAMILY FIT

Like many of you, I grew up watching television shows like "Leave It to Beaver," "Ozzie and Harriet," "Father Knows Best," and "The Donna Reed Show." I still enjoy them. But I have one complaint: They all seem the same!

I'm not echoing the complaint made by many media critics who condemn these old shows because they depicted traditional, two-parent families. I'm glad they did. Instead, my complaint is that the parents and kids all seemed to act the same in these shows. To put it in the language of this book, they displayed the same behavioral style.

Think about it. Whether the families were the Cleavers, Nelsons, Andersons, or Stones, both parents and children seemed to be steadfast, predictable, sincere, easygoing, and people-oriented. They were high "S" individuals. The mothers also showed a higher amount of "C" behavior; their homes were always immaculate and perfectly organized.

Everyone in these families seemed to fit together like peas in a pod. When they experienced conflict or when the kids got into trouble, the parents calmly worked through the problem and found a solution—all in thirty minutes.

Now that Karen and I are parents, we've noticed that our sitcom parenting role models of the past don't seem to work too well. It's not just that Karen refuses to imitate June and Donna by wearing a dress and pearls as she cooks dinner. In the Boyd household, family feuds seem much more intense and harder to resolve.

The reality is that any home consists of several different people. As you've worked through this book, you've probably discovered that you and your spouse have different behavioral styles, and each of you is different in some way from each of your children. Each of us has our own likes and dislikes. We have different emotions and energy levels. Some of us are intense. Others are more laid back. We see things differently and hear different things when we're listening to the same story.

Writer Anne Cassidy put it this way in an article in *Family Circle* magazine:

> Real families are more like a handful of snowflakes: Each person is different, and some are more different than others. But that doesn't mean they can't all get along. Happy families happen when there's respect for the uniqueness of each and every member.[1]

I suspect that John Wilmot, the Earl of Rochester back in the seventeenth century, felt some of the strain of different behavioral styles clashing in his household when he made the following remark: "Before I got married I had six theories about bringing up children; now I have six children and no theories."

What parent has not experienced the reality of that statement? Nothing leaves us less "all knowing" than having to deal with children on a daily basis—especially when we have children we don't relate to well or can't quite figure out.

## HOW'S YOUR FIT?

Up to this point, I've helped you understand your behavioral style as well as those of your kids. I've given you a few brief tips on how to deal with "D," "I," "S," and "C" children.

Now it's time to give you solid, practical pointers on how to raise a child according to the design God gave him. The first question to consider is: How well do you fit with your kids?

This subject has been thoroughly researched by Dr. Stellas Chess and Dr. Alexander Thomas. In their book, *Know Your Child,* they discuss the parent-child relationship in terms of "goodness of fit."[2] This occurs when each member of a family feels he blends well with the rest of the family. When parents adjust their demands and expectations to make them compatible with a child's temperament, abilities, and character traits, the child feels he fits. A good fit can enhance a child's strengths and help overcome natural limitations and vulnerabilities.

"Poorness of fit," on the other hand, occurs when parents treat every child the same, making no adjustments in their leadership style. With such a fit, the child is likely to experience excessive stress, and that can jeopardize healthy development.

A parent who is active and adventurous may repeatedly push and demand too much from a quiet, passive, stay-at-home child. A cautious parent may unnecessarily restrict the adventurous, risk-taking behavior in a very active child.

An "S" child may be born to a parent who demands perfection and is unable to give the child affirmation, affection, and unconditional love. An easily distracted "I" child may develop a problem if his parents insist that he concentrate on a task for a long period of time without a break. A parent who enjoys sudden, unplanned change may compound the insecurities of a child who needs time to warm up to change.

### DIFFERENT KIDS, DIFFERENT FITS

How well does your parenting style fit with each one of your children? If you have more than one child, you may already have discovered that you fit with one child and not with another. This is not uncommon.

Tina's first child, Nathan, was what you would call an easy child. From the day she brought him home from the hospital, they seemed to click. She understood his moods and was in tune with his rhythms. When he cried, she could tell whether the cause was a wet diaper, hunger, or pain, and she knew what to do.

But when Lauren, her second child, came along, things were very different. Lauren was much more demanding than Nathan, and when she cried, Tina couldn't seem to calm her.

As an infant, Lauren was harder to pacify. As a toddler, she was much more energetic and active. Today, as a teenager, she continues to assert her individuality.

Tina never understood why she seemed to fit with Nathan better than Lauren until she understood their behavioral styles. Both Tina and Nathan score high in the "S" category, while Lauren is a "D." So it's natural that Tina understands Nathan better—he's more like her! What she needs to do is learn how to adjust her natural style as she works with each child. And she's doing it. She now appreciates her daughter's strong personality, even though it still can make waves in their laid-back family.

In our family, Karen and I also noticed differences right from the start. We realized early on that we would have to make adjustments.

Chad, our first child, is a high "D," with a lot of the "I" style mixed in. Even as a toddler, he rarely slept through the night. He would wake up ready to go at 5:00 A.M. He demanded our attention and didn't play well by himself.

I remember putting Chad in bed one evening when he was about twenty-two months old. I prayed with him, walked out the door to my easy chair, and before I could pick up the television remote control, there he was. I took him back to bed and told him to stay there, but in less than a minute he was back.

This maddening routine continued for over an hour. I finally began to walk out of his room, then step immediately to the side so that I could reach down to catch Chad on his way out. Talk about determination!

But I was also determined not to lose that battle, and through persistence I finally got the message across—only to repeat the whole thing the next night.

This type of child is what James Dobson and other family experts call a "strong willed," "difficult," or "stubborn" child. Others have labeled them "mother killers"!

Then Kristi came along. She was quiet, reserved, compliant, and fairly independent. We would sometimes "lose" her. We knew she hadn't gone outside, so we would search throughout our home and finally find her hidden away in some closet, playing with her dolls or lining up Micromachines in a parade. As she grew older, Kristi kept her room in perfect order. She has her way of doing things—the right way.

When Chad was a baby, I'd lie on the couch with him on my chest. I'd bounce up and down until he finally fell asleep. I tried this with Kristi as a baby, but she wanted no part of it. She would wiggle and squirm, and was quite content being placed in her crib to go to sleep by herself.

Our daughter Callie is different as well. She shows a mixture of traits. She will play by herself, but she also is a couch potato like her dad. She loves to sit in my lap and watch television or read—anything as long as she's sitting with me. She's loving and affectionate, but she also can be obstinate at times.

So each child is unique, and the differences show up in many situations.

The other night I heard an awful scream in the kitchen. I thought Callie had cut off her finger with a knife or something, so I rushed in and found all three kids dancing around screaming, "Tarantula! Tarantula!" A tiny spider was crawling up the wall, and they were swatting at it and spraying it with deodorant.

I'm the official bug killer in our home. Karen and the kids find them; I kill them. I even have a beeper so I can maintain a twenty-four-hour bug alert. Confronted by this spider, I took off my shoe, reached up, and smashed the thing. Blood and guts went everywhere.

Chad, my high "D" son, said, "Way to go, Dad!"

Callie ("S") said, "Is it really dead, Daddy?"

Kristi ("C") said, "You know, you shouldn't kill one of God's creatures. You should have thrown him outside."

Karen ("C/S") said, "Look what you've done! Look at that awful mess!"

And I ("D/I") said to Karen, "Ah, yes, a mess. That's your jurisdiction."

## MANAGING OUR FAMILIES

Karen and I have come to realize that, for our family to experience the harmony and unity God desires, we need to make some important adjustments in our natural parenting styles as we raise each child. Flexing is essential to reducing the chaos in your home and allowing your child to develop healthy self-esteem.

Psalm 133:1 says, "How good and pleasant it is when brothers live together in unity!" But this bliss does not drop out of heaven into our homes. We have to work at it. It is difficult for families full of different personalities to make a good fit when they don't know why they disagree so often. They need to learn how to manage different people differently.

The Bible teaches us to manage our families well. A passage about people eligible for leadership in the church, 1 Timothy 3:4-5, clearly expresses the importance of family management: "He must manage his own family well and see that his children obey him with proper respect. (If anyone does not know how to manage his own family, how can he take care of God's church?)" That's a good question.

In a working situation, a good manager should be able to discern the needs and motivations of each person working under him. He adjusts his leadership style with each individual in order to get the most out of that employee. One person may need constant attention and encouragement, while another simply needs a challenging project and the freedom to do it his way.

In his book, *13 Fatal Errors Managers Make, and How to Avoid Them,* W. Steven Brown lists "Manage Everyone the Same Way" as fatal error number five. "The manager who tries to manage everyone on his staff the same way, using only one technique, can prepare himself for disappointments," Brown writes. "He will never be successful (and probably will wonder why). The successful manager grasps hold of the essential differences in the personalities of those on his staff and, aware of their strengths and weaknesses, manages them as individuals."[3]

Effective family managers must practice the same principle. Understanding the differing behavior styles of your family members will assist you in managing your family.

## ADJUSTING YOUR PARENTING STYLE

The very thought of adapting your parenting style to different children may seem impossible. After all, isn't it your "natural" style? It's important to realize that I do not mean becoming a different person. You cannot change your basic, God-given nature. But you can voluntarily and temporarily adjust your behavior in order to meet other people's needs, to build a mutually satisfying relationship.

Many people simply need to understand another person's behavioral style. Then, *if they find they need to make adjustments, they manage to do it.*

Other people may be able to make the adjustments but are not willing to do so. Perhaps they are too selfish to make the necessary commitment to develop a mature relationship. Perhaps they're lazy. Either way, the relationship moves toward isolation and a feeling of emotional distance.

Still others are willing to make adjustments, but are not able to. It may be that something in their background is preventing them from expressing the kind of love another family member needs. Or they may lack emotional maturity or training in social skills. These people may need extra help, or even counseling.

But if you are reading this book, you probably are willing to give it a try. If that's the case, I have some suggestions for how to adjust your parenting style:

*1. Recognize how your personal perceptions confuse, color, or cloud critical people issues.* Most problems in human relations stem from a difference in perception—two or more people viewing the same situation in different ways.

Your perceptions about your children will be influenced by your needs and values, your self-concept, past experiences, prejudices, likes, and dislikes. And, yes, it will be influenced by your behavioral style. In some cases these personal perceptions can be helpful. If you believe what the Bible says about the natural selfishness of human beings, this value will influence how you approach your two young children when they are fighting over which television show to watch, and each gives a different story about whose turn it is to choose.

These perceptions can also hinder you. In some cases, your behavioral style will prevent you from understanding the true nature of a conflict. Your perceptions can prevent you from responding properly to different situations. They influence your expectations of what you want from your children and from others. Mostly, they prevent you from understanding why others behave as they do.

Bill's natural Directive style, which serves him so well as chief executive officer in a west coast Fortune 500 company, doesn't work so well with his ten-year-old son, Kirk. A high "I," Kirk thrives on people interaction, rather than completing tasks.

At home, Bill has come up with a list of daily chores for Kirk to complete. He directs Kirk like he directs people at the office. Bill wants to tell

Kirk what to do, and then he expects Kirk to finish the job on his own. After all, that's how Bill operates. He likes it when his own boss tells him what to do and then gets out of the way.

So Bill is frustrated and angry with Kirk when he arrives home from work to find chores unfinished. He thinks Kirk is irresponsible and needs to quit goofing off with his friends. What he doesn't realize is that Kirk needs and wants to do more things *with* his dad. He wants the work to be fun.

Interacting with his dad is a high priority on Kirk's internal "to-do" list. He may even purposely misbehave or manipulate the circumstance in order to force his dad to help him. Even if he's punished, at least he's receiving some attention from his father.

*2. Learn to view your child in terms of his strengths rather than his limitations.* The natural tendency is just the opposite, to view people in terms of their limitations. Because their perspectives and behavior are not like yours, you naturally think your way is the "right" way.

For example, a high "I" dad may think his high "C" daughter spends too much time thinking and reading. Rather than see her thinking ability as a strength, he may view her as too analytical and removed from the world of people. A high "C" mom who likes to keep her home in perfect order may be totally exasperated with a high "S" son who doesn't seem to care about cleanliness "like he should." These parents find themselves criticizing their children constantly.

As I'll discuss in chapter 15, many married people develop the same problem. They focus on the negatives in their spouses rather than the positives. These couples will find it helpful to look at how their personalities and behavioral styles blend together and give them added strength.

So it is for parents. Becoming a student of your child also means that *you* can learn from your child. Have you ever considered the possibility that God may have given your children strengths that could help you and your family? For many parents (especially those with very young children), this is an incredible thought. That's because they haven't looked far enough into the future.

Let's say you are a high "S" mom, and you are having problems with your six-year-old, high "D" son. Right now he's demanding and energetic, and he wears you out. But consider this: Suppose your son is now seventeen, and both you and your husband come down with a virus and are laid up in bed for a solid week. Someone needs to take charge of the household—cooking meals and buying groceries and making sure all the kids get off to school on time.

Suddenly you see your son in a different light. You need for him to utilize his directive style. You need his energy. But if you spent years criticizing your son's behavioral style, he may lack the confidence or desire to step in and help now that he's needed.

3. *Adjust your approach to relate to your child according to his needs, not yours.* Learn what encourages your child, what motivates him, and how to communicate with him. You cannot assume that he should be treated the way you prefer to be treated.

Earlier in this chapter, I talked about Bill, the high "D" businessman who doesn't understand his high "I" son, Kirk. Bill needs to adjust his parenting style to include more Interactive parenting behavior in certain situations. Kirk needs to learn how to do his chores on his own, but Bill may need to step in and help Kirk do them for a while. This would give Kirk the experience of completing a task, which is important to Bill, while also giving him time with his dad.

Bill may struggle with his natural fear that Kirk is taking advantage of him. He'll need to make a conscious decision to set that fear aside, knowing that Kirk is not manipulating his father but merely operating from his natural behavioral style.

Christine is a single-parent, high "I" mother who loves to participate in social activities. Her weekends are filled with action. Her son, Mark, a high "C" who enjoys being alone, needs time to adjust to change and to new people. He may welcome one social gathering per weekend, but his mom's schedule produces a great deal of stress.

Christine doesn't understand why Mark prefers to spend less time with people than she does. She thinks he's anti-social. "All he wants to do is stay at home and read books or play with a couple of friends on his street. If he doesn't get out and meet people, he's going to be a boring kid who misses out on life."

Mark has suffered from severe headaches during the past year, but Christine doesn't yet see the connection. She thinks the best way to relieve his stress is to get him interacting with people. After all, that works for her.

All children need to develop the confidence to adapt to strange settings and new social experiences. Christine probably needs to push Mark to get him more involved with people, but she also needs to recognize his behavioral style and let him move at his own pace. As difficult as it will be for her, she needs to slow down and cut back on the number of social gatherings she attends. Over time, Mark will feel capable of confronting change, even though his immediate emotional reaction may be uncomfortable.

## CHRIST'S EXAMPLE

This concept of adjusting your style to meet another person's needs was modeled by our Lord. In John 11, we find the account of the death and resurrection of Lazarus. While Lazarus was still sick, Martha and Mary, his sisters, sent word for Jesus to come. Jesus remained where He was. By the time Jesus finally made His way to Bethany, Lazarus had died.

When Martha, who was probably a fast-paced, task-oriented woman, heard that Jesus was coming, she went out to meet him. Mary, who was slower-paced and more people-oriented, remained in the house.

Martha made her thoughts very clear: "Lord, if you had been here, my brother would not have died." In the verses following, Jesus reasoned with her and confronted her with a challenging question.

After this, Martha went into the house and told Mary that Jesus had arrived. When Mary went to Jesus, she said exactly the same thing Martha had said earlier: "Lord, if you had been here, my brother would not have died."

Jesus did not respond to Mary with a challenge. Instead, He showed great compassion. As He saw her weeping, the text says that Jesus "was deeply moved in spirit and troubled." He asked, "Where have you laid him?" and together they walked to the tomb. Then comes the shortest verse in the Bible: "Jesus wept."

Two different people asked the same question, but Jesus responded to them differently. Martha (high "D") needed a challenge. Mary (high "S") needed compassion. Jesus' model of adjusting His style to meet other people's needs forms the basis of godly parenting.

## FAMILY FIT CHARTS

To help you learn how to adjust your behavioral style to the needs of your children, at the conclusion of this chapter are several pages of charts. If you are a high "S" parent, for example, you'll find information on how to fit with a high "D" child.

For each parent-child combination, you'll find information in three categories:

*Strengths:* When similarities and differences are understood, accepted, and appreciated, every parent-child blend has certain advantages.

*Struggles:* Each pair also has natural points of conflict. These conflicts center around issues such as pace, priority, perspective, decision-making, communication, and handling change.

*Strategies:* When the natural dynamics of each combination is understood, specific steps can be taken that lead to a good parent-child fit.

In my workshops and seminars, I've seen time and again that parents experience an immediate "Ah-ha" when they understand style similarities and differences between themselves and their children. As they become aware of the natural strengths and struggles in their parent-child blends, they become more willing to flex their parenting style.

"Now I understand why my wife and my fourteen-year-old daughter fight and argue all the time. They're both 'D's,' " said one father. "But what complicates things even more is that I'm a high 'D' as well! Three people, all wanting control!"

A mother described herself and her husband as "rather intense" people. But she was always puzzled by her son. "Until now, we have never understood why we can't seem to get our son motivated. It's not that he is a bad kid; he's really quite helpful and pleasant to be around. He seldom gives us a hard time about anything. But we just can't seem to get him to take initiative."

As you read through the charts, remember the following:

1. *Each parent/child match is unique.* If you are an "I" and your child a "C," the statements on the chart should help, but they may not always perfectly apply to your situation. The information is not intended to provide a magic formula that will fix your relationship. These charts will help you understand the dynamic that naturally exists between you and your child and give you suggestions to experiment with.

2. *Certain combinations may be more prone to push you into an ineffective parenting style* (e.g., autocratic, permissive, accommodating, perfectionistic). Becoming more aware of your hot buttons can help you remain in your effective parenting style and also flex your natural style to incorporate the positive qualities of the other styles, when necessary.

Read the pairings that correspond to your family first. Remember to read the other categories if you or your child express more than one dominant style. As you work through these charts, reflect on questions such as these: What is true and what is not true in these relationships? What issues need immediate attention and action? How are we alike? How are we different? Where do we fit together easily and where do sparks fly?

Also, I suggest you explain the principles of style to each of your children and read through the charts that apply to your specific parent/child match. Think of specific illustrations and times when the strengths and struggles have been clearly observed. Let your children offer possible solutions, opinions, and suggestions on how to implement the strategies. Get everyone involved in becoming more family fit.

Now is the time to begin focusing on your child and discovering how to work with his particular style on an everyday basis. Remember, these are *guidelines,* not *givens*. Neat formulas are always tempting, but life is not that simple, especially when it comes to parent/child interplay. Take what applies and use it. Leave the rest. Only you can truly know what applies to you and your child.

## NOTES

1. Anne Cassidy, "Family Fit," *Family Circle* (February 1991): 89.

2. Stellas Chess and Alexander Thomas, *Know Your Child* (New York: Basic Books, 1987).

3. W. Steven Brown, *13 Fatal Errors Managers Make, and How to Avoid Them* (Old Tappan, N.J.: Fleming H. Revell Company, 1985), 62.

# DETERMINED ("D") CHILD

*Strengths:* As long as you both share the same desires and direction, you will experience harmony, and you'll be able to accomplish much as a team. Your mutual goals, admiration, and desire to get results can be very positive and affirming.

*Struggles:* Power struggles over control are the most frequent source of friction and fighting. Since you both are competitive, you both want to win every battle at all costs; neither will want to give in or give up. You think, *If I give an inch, he will take a mile,* and in many cases you're right. But if you cannot reach compromises, your home life can become a battleground.

*Strategies:* • Don't force issues. Don't threaten or give ultimatums. • Balance holding a hard line with allowing your child some areas over which he can have control. • Give the child choices whenever possible. For example: "Would you like to clean your room now or when you finish watching that television show?" • Do not lecture. • When possible, give direct, one-word commands: "Sarah, the *room!*" • Discuss with your child areas of greatest disruption. Sit down together, set down some working rules, and stick to them. This trains the child to become responsible and to understand limits. Don't argue with this child. If you do, he has won the battle, because he was able to control your emotions and reactions.

# INFLUENCING ("I") CHILD

*Strengths:* Both of you are confident and enjoy a fast-paced approach to life. Your child will want to please you so desperately that he will follow (or at least appear to follow) your leadership.

*Struggles:* Your desire to accomplish goals and get results can easily be frustrated by the "take-life-as-it-comes" attitude of this child. Frequent conflicts may occur when your focus on getting things done clashes with the child's focus on having fun and being with his friends. Also, the child's tendency toward disorganization and not completing tasks can cause you to become very angry.

*Strategies:* • Realize that this child may never have your focus or your goal orientation, but this doesn't make him bad. • Make work fun. Do some chores and projects *with* your child. • Provide ideas for transforming talk into action. Write down the details of what you expect and keep rules simple and easy to follow. • Listen enthusiastically to your child's long stories and tales. This is a skill to be encouraged—he'll probably end up making a living by using his mouth. • Give a lot of praise, affection, and approval. • Accept the child's feelings and emotions, as well as insisting on facts. • Your strength to stand firm and alone under pressure can provide an excellent role model for this child, whose greatest struggle tends be succumbing to peer pressure.

# SOFT-HEARTED ("S") CHILD

*Strengths:* You like to lead and this child likes to follow. He will feel secure with you as long as you show controlled, stable behavior.

*Struggles:* If you come on too strong, this child will easily be intimidated and will take it personally. Also, hard-charging "D" parents often misunderstand the soft-hearted, easygoing "S" child and label him "weak." This can easily lead to self-esteem problems for the child.

*Strategies:* • Do not expect the child to figure out how to accomplish a task. Spell out, step by step, exactly what to do. He wants to please you, so he wants to know how you want something done. • Watch how you say things. This child is very sensitive and can be easily hurt by spontaneous, off-the-cuff negative comments and anger. • Do not push him into heated competition. • Never compare the child to anyone else. This is demotivating for him and can cause him to give up trying. • Soft-hearted children need to feel close to their parents. To give your child a sense of belonging and acceptance, you must make a special effort to spend time with the child and give plenty of affection.

# CONSCIENTIOUS ("C") CHILD

*Strengths:* Since both of you focus on tasks and enjoy working independently, you share some common ground. As a team, with your direction and the child's attention to detail, you can accomplish a lot.

*Struggles:* You tend to jump into a project quickly, whereas the child likes to think things through in detail. You both want results, but the child wants things done right and you want things done *now*. This difference in pace is a chief source of conflict. Also, your tendency to control things can be discouraging to this child who does not want to feel pressured.

*Strategies:* • Do not become impatient with the child. Don't rush or push him. • Give him time to make decisions. • Allow the child time to gather all the facts and do things "correctly"—as he defines "correct." • Be careful with criticism. While it may motivate you, he may internalize the criticism deeply, and it may seriously damage his self-esteem. Callous comments or acts of aggression will immobilize him. • Be prepared to answer the child's "why" questions and provide in-depth explanations patiently. • Accept and affirm his cautious nature. Do not expect him to be a risk-taker like you. • Listen to your child. His reasons for doing what he does are usually thought out thoroughly.

# DETERMINED ("D") CHILD

*Strengths:* The Interactive parent will delight in the strengths of their "D" children, brag about their accomplishments, and share the spotlight in any honors. Both parent and child possess confident, activity-driven outlooks on life and want to look like winners. The "I" parent's frequent praise for achievement and encouragement is motivating to the "D" child, who desires to be admired.

*Struggles:* Interactive parents want to be liked by their children and have a tendency to become too permissive. While "D" children need some freedom and choices, they must have well-defined and firmly adhered to boundaries. If the high "I" parent is not careful, the "D" child will take control of the home.

*Strategies:* • Set clearly defined limits and boundaries and stick to them. When rules are broken and lines are crossed, you must follow through with previously determined consequences and discipline. • Remember: This child tends to take advantage of any inconsistency or lack of follow-through on your part. He is determined to take over whenever possible. • Do not be afraid of confrontation. Expect it. • When correcting, be brief and to the point. "D" children do not want or need long-winded explanations. Give him one word commands and expect him to obey. • Realize that this child will frequently push you out of your comfort zone and that this may be emotionally draining to you.

# INFLUENCING ("I") CHILD

*Strengths:* Both of you live life enthusiastically and optimistically, enjoy being with people, like to have fun, want to impress others, and freely give compliments and praise. In fact, you can become a mutual admiration society. When you make mistakes, you both will give a lot of slack and tend to forgive easily.

*Struggles:* Because both parent and child tend to live life emotionally, you may end up competing to be the center of attention. Jealousy between a high "I" teenage daughter and mother is not uncommon. Also, since you both tend to be impulsive, issues such as following through on responsibilities and financial discipline can become a major family problem.

*Strategies:* • Remember to listen to your "I" child. He likes to talk as much as you. • Realize that your tendency to be overly permissive may help produce an even greater lack of responsibility in this child. Learn to incorporate some of the strengths of both the Directive and Corrective parenting styles in order to give balance to your natural parenting style. • Realize that this child dislikes details as much as you do. Write down who is responsible for what. You can make this fun by turning it into a game. • Set limits and boundaries and follow through with discipline. Resist bailing the child out when he fails to follow through. This will not be easy, but it is necessary in order for him to grow into a competent, responsible adult.

# SOFT-HEARTED ("S") CHILD

*Strengths:* Interactive parents will appreciate the easygoing, relaxed nature of the Soft-hearted child. The parent likes to talk; the child enjoys listening. They tend to get along very well together.

*Struggles:* At the same time, most struggles between "I" parents and "S" children center around differences in pace. The high "I" parent enjoys a fast-paced, exciting lifestyle, and this is exactly what the high "S" wants to avoid. The high "I" likes noise and confusion; the high "S" desires quiet. The high "I" parent thrives on spontaneity, variety, and quick changes. The high "S" child is slow to change, enjoys routines, and dislikes surprises and unplanned changes.

*Strategies:* • Slow down your approach. Let him respond at his own slower pace. • Allow him time for making decisions. • Tone down your enthusiasm. Don't embarrass him by being overly enthusiastic about his achievements in front of others. Provide support and encouragement in private, rather than public, ways. • Be sincere in your praise and appreciation of him. • Accept his shyness and the fact that he may be slow to warm up to new people and events. • Whenever possible, give advance warning as to what and how things may change. • Ask more questions and listen carefully to his answers. • Ask for his help in getting tasks accomplished. The "S" child loves to feel that his contribution is valued and wanted.

# CONSCIENTIOUS ("C") CHILD

*Strengths:* You can learn much from each other, as each of your strengths provide a good balance to the other's weaknesses. The child can learn not to take things so seriously and to have more fun. And your child can help you think things through in a more analytical way.

*Struggles:* Your differences can lead to frequent misunderstandings. You love to talk, but sometimes your child needs to have time alone. Also, because you are so verbal, you may miss the child's more indirect way of sharing concerns.

*Strategies:* • Listen so you will better understand. Be alert to subtle nuances in what the child says. He uses words sparingly, and every word has meaning. • Tone down your emotional reactions and your enthusiasm. Be more factual and objective, especially in the midst of conflict. • Realize that the child's drive for perfection is as deeply felt as your need for fun. He cannot simply "lighten up" and laugh off mistakes. • Allow him time alone to be disappointed when his work doesn't measure up to his standards. • Don't rush or push. Allow him time alone to do quality work. • Be sincere in your praise and appreciation of his work. Tell him what he did well in specific descriptive terms, rather than simply saying "Great job!" "Terrific!" or "You did a fantastic job." • Remember, his worst fear is criticism of his work. Be gentle when correcting. • Don't expect him to be a risk-taker. Accept his cautious nature.

# DETERMINED ("D") CHILD

*Strengths:* You have the ability to provide the encouragement on which this child thrives as he seeks to achieve his goals and exert leadership.

*Struggles:* Since the child desires constant control and instant action, he can easily exhaust a parent like you, who wants things to stay calm and peaceful. The biggest problem with this combination comes in the area of discipline. You tend to be too lenient, wanting to avoid conflict, and he knows it. He can easily take advantage of you. You want peace at all costs, and the long-term result can be an uncontrollable child.

*Strategies:* • The child needs some areas over which he has control. Just make sure *you* are not controlled by him. And don't become disheartened when he doesn't need you for some activity. He likes to do things himself. Don't take it personally. • Be firm. Force yourself to take a stand. Make strong statements and establish your authority. • Be decisive and stick to your decisions. Realize that you will be tested. It's important that you do not waver. • Also, understand that being more directive will not be easy for you, but it is necessary. • Don't feel like you are a failure because your child is so different from you. He's the way he is because of his design.

# INFLUENCING ("I") CHILD

*Strengths:* You have the potential to get along well. You love to have a good time and the child can provide the entertainment. Both provide praise and appreciation which both need to feel good about themselves.

*Struggles:* Keeping up with the pace of this child can be a challenge for you. Your child likes change and moves from activity to activity like a tornado. You prefer things to be calm, peaceful, and routine.

*Strategies:* • You must be firm and set limits with this child. His persuasive, fast talking ability can leave you speechless, wondering why you gave permission for some activity. • Don't overdo for this child. He tends to dislike work and will let you do everything for him if you are not careful. This can breed irresponsibility into the child; he'll go through life thinking someone else will take care of him, so he can coast along and have fun. • Don't bail him out when he has not been responsible with homework or keeping on a schedule. Let him experience the logical consequences of being disorganized or forgetful. • Help him become more organized by writing down how something is to be done in a step-by-step manner. Use "To-Do" lists, but don't be surprised when this child frequently loses the list.

# SOFT-HEARTED ("S") CHILD

*Strengths:* You have a lot in common and can enjoy being with each other. Both of you appreciate a relaxed, calm, peaceful home atmosphere, and work to keep things that way. You both help each other out. The two of you enjoy "do nothing" times—spending the afternoon watching television, wandering through a shopping mall, or killing time in a boat fishing—without concern for time or telephone.

*Struggles:* The biggest trouble comes in the area of communication. You both talk indirectly—both will suggest things, but neither will want to make decisions. Also, neither wants to initiate anything that might result in change. If you are too accommodating, the child may become too dependent upon you and grow up lacking the ability for independent thinking and doing. Also, since neither of you wants to upset the other, hurt feelings can be suppressed. Over time, this unwillingness to bring up unpleasant issues can become a problem.

*Strategies:* • Balance doing things for your child with encouraging him to do things for himself. • Initiate more and be more decisive. • Realize that some conflict and change is healthy. Life constantly changes, so don't overprotect your child from this reality. • Draw out how your child feels and honestly share how you feel. Don't sweep hurt or negative feelings under the rug, hoping they will go away.

# CONSCIENTIOUS ("C") CHILD

*Strengths:* Both of you tend to be slower-paced, allow one another "alone time," and can enjoy being together without a lot of conversation. Neither is pushy, and you both prefer to avoid conflict.

*Struggles:* In this pair, the critical nature of your child can easily result in hurt feelings on the part of the parent. You will tend to suppress those feelings rather than talk about them. The child's inner, intuitive, logical approach to life can at times clash with your more feelings-oriented focus. Also, you naturally work to develop close relationships, and you may feel concern about the child's cool, calculated manner.

*Strategies:* • Recognize this child's need for privacy. If there is a conflict, give him time alone to think, and ask to talk about the problem later. • He needs private time to recharge after stress. Do not interpret this as rejection. • Don't push this child into closeness. Choose your sharing times carefully. Talk about how you feel and listen for understanding when you sense the child has withdrawn and shut down. • Be prepared to give in-depth explanations in a patient manner. • Allow him time for disappointment when he has not met his own high standards. • Give sincere, descriptive praise, and show appreciation for his work. • Don't overreact to his tendency to be critical, but gently guide him to accept shortcomings in himself and others.

# DETERMINED ("D") CHILD

*Strengths:* Both parent and child share a similar bent toward accomplishing tasks. As long as they share these goals they can be very effective as a pair, and mutually helpful.

*Struggles:* If parent and child have opposing goals, the "C" parent will find himself in a hopeless battle. The "C" wants things done "right," according to *his* standards. But "right" to a "D" is seldom as complicated as the "C" seems to make it. The "D" child simply wants to do it his way and get it done. The child will tend to make decisions and do things quickly, and miss key details that are important to the "C" parent.

*Strategies:* • Give your "D" child some responsibility, and keep yourself from stepping in to try to make things better. He needs to be in charge of something. • Be lavish in affirming the goals and accomplishments of this child. This may not come naturally for you, since you often see how something can be done just a little bit better. • Recognize that risk-taking is important to this child. Set limits according to wisdom and safety. • Accept that life with a "D" child will be one change and challenge after another. • Recognize this child's need for physical activity. • Try not to argue with him; your reasoning may not be convincing. • Most of all, don't expect perfection. Be cautious about setting your standards so high that your child feels he will never be able to reach them. Even a "D" will quit trying if he is constantly criticized for not measuring up.

# INFLUENCING ("I") CHILD

*Strengths:* Your love for detail and doing things right is exactly what this child needs to be more balanced and successful in life. And your child can be a source of freshness and joy to you, because you tend to be more serious.

*Struggles:* Since you are on opposite ends of the "pace and priority" continuum, you may find it difficult to understand this child's persistent, intense need for fun. Because of your high standards, the child may not receive the praise and approval he needs. This may cause him to look for approval from other people.

*Strategies:* • You must modify your expectations for this child. Realize that he will never give the same attention to details that you do. • This child hungers for acceptance and approval, so look for strengths and praise him at every opportunity. • Enjoy your child for who he is, even though his strengths may be different from yours. • Stop working on your projects and tasks long enough to give the child your focused attention. • Listen enthusiastically to his stories and tales. It energizes him to talk and have you listen attentively. • Most of all, don't push for perfection. Don't set your standards so high that your child comes to feel he will never be able to reach them.

# SOFT-HEARTED ("S") CHILD

*Strengths:* Both parent and child take things slowly and can enjoy a more reserved, low-key relationship. The parent will appreciate the "S" child's easygoing, agreeable nature that avoids noisy conflicts.

*Struggles:* You may be frustrated when the child doesn't think through things the way you do, or share your enthusiasm for key details. You also may worry about why you cannot seem to motivate this child to strive for the same standards of excellence by which you operate.

*Strategies:* • Be aware of your tendency to focus on critical tasks and doing things correctly. Balance your interaction by exploring how your child feels and what is going on in his world. • Be more open and share your feelings with your child. Draw him out. • Allow your child the luxury of simply doing nothing at times. This is how he recharges his batteries. • Remember to explain how you want something done. Do not expect this child to figure out all the details by himself. • Show sincere appreciation for any effort, even if it does not come up to your standards. • Be careful with your criticism. Criticism can sound harsh, even if you don't intend it to be. • Most of all, don't set your standards so high that your child feels he will never be able to reach them. The child will feel inadequate and not valued, and he will simply give up.

# CONSCIENTIOUS ("C") CHILD

*Strengths:* This is a natural combination to produce a child prodigy. You can enjoy working hard together on some task or project and give full attention to what needs to be done. You both are prone to seriousness. And both parent and child are dedicated to quality, excellence, and doing things the right way.

*Struggles:* The trouble comes when parent and child disagree on whose way is the "right" way. Both can quickly shut down and withdraw to plan their next move. And both tend to wage a war of indirect communication.

*Strategies:* • Be open at times if your child suggests a different way of doing something. Be willing to flex on some of your standards to finish a job in a mutually acceptable way. • Be careful when you correct your child. You well know that criticism of *your* work is one of *your* greatest fears. • Don't overreact when your child criticizes you. • Show plenty of affection and emotion. Like you, this child needs to feel loved and valued, and he may not be naturally affectionate. • Most of all, don't set your standards so high that your child feels he will never be able to reach them.

CHAPTER TEN

# "MIRROR, MIRROR . . ."

When Suzanne walked into a party, she instantly became the center of attention. She was beautiful, vivacious, and she said the most scandalous things to shock people. Yes, Suzanne was the one everyone wanted to know, and for someone who lived and worked in Hollywood during the "Golden Age" of the 1930s and 1940s, that could be a heady experience.

As long as she could remember, her life had revolved around show business. Her mother had worked as a dancer in vaudeville for many years. Her cousins worked in the theater and in the movie studios.

Suzanne didn't get along with her mother very well. Perhaps she never forgave her for leaving to perform around the country with her new husband—leaving eight-year-old Suzanne behind in an orphanage. Four years later her mother retrieved her, but they fought bitterly during Suzanne's teenage years.

Suzanne became a chorus girl, appearing in several movies. Then she became a dance captain at a popular nightclub—one of those frequented by all the top producers and directors. It was here that she received her first lesson in the dark side of Hollywood; the owner of this nightclub had strong connections to the Mafia.

These were dangerous years. Suzanne was threatened by mobsters when she refused to date them. She knew the girls who went out with these men, and she knew the ones who disappeared.

Eventually Suzanne found a new outlet for her drive and ambition. She became a director's assistant. With her intelligence and forceful personality, she performed well. Directors began asking for her services, and she learned the business of making movies.

Suzanne's ultimate goal was to become a producer, a deal maker. Today, women like her are making millions of dollars in Hollywood. But in the 1940s, nobody took her seriously. She felt thwarted by her peers, by the industry, by men. Her career began to go sour—a bitter pill for someone with so much ambition.

Then, at the age of thirty-nine, Suzanne was given a chance to start a new life. She married a movie studio carpenter. Soon she gave birth to a baby girl.

Suzanne decided she would not allow her daughter, Cathy, to endure the pain and failure she herself had experienced. This girl would not go into show business. She would grow up to be a wife and mother. Suzanne would be her role model.

The problem was that Suzanne never had much of a role model herself for raising a child. She loved her daughter, but she didn't know what to do. In the process of creating this new life for herself and her child, she nearly destroyed them both.

As Cathy grew up, Suzanne began to sense how similar they were. Cathy shared her mother's intelligence, her forceful personality, and her ability to get along with people. Whereas many parents want to make their children just like themselves, Suzanne reacted *negatively* when Cathy behaved like her.

Cathy loved to dance. When she was a child, she would put records of Broadway musicals on the phonograph, pull back the living room furniture, and dance to all the songs. For years she begged her mother to allow her to take dance lessons, but Suzanne refused. Her daughter was not going to be a dancer, period. She could participate in Girl Scouts and in church activities.

To keep Cathy from experiencing failure, Suzanne kept her from trying anything new or risky. As a teenager, Cathy decided she wanted to be a stunt girl in the movies. So Suzanne brought home a stunt woman she had known at the studio, and for two hours they argued with Cathy about this "foolish idea." As Cathy recalls, "That was always what I heard when I told her I wanted to try something, 'Oh, that's just too hard to get into.' She didn't want me to be hurt as she was hurt herself."

Over the years, Suzanne tried to repress any hint of behavior which did not fit the role she had chosen for her daughter. She demeaned her intelligence and always called her "Dumb bunny." She wanted Cathy to believe she was stupid, that she couldn't take care of herself, that she needed a husband to meet her needs.

"She wanted me to be safe," Cathy says. "And the one way that she could accomplish this was to destroy my self-esteem. Whenever I showed any inclination to take matters into my own hands, to take initiative, it was always squashed."

Their relationship was strained from the beginning, but it deteriorated into all-out warfare during Cathy's teenage years. "I would go into my room and think of the meanest things I could say to her, and she would do the same to me."

All the years of pain and failure caught up with Suzanne, and she began turning to alcohol and barbiturates. At age nineteen, Cathy married an Air Force Academy graduate, and Suzanne put on a lavish wedding. It was her dream come true.

Within two years, Cathy separated from her husband, and Suzanne lay dying in the hospital. Cathy still recalls one day when she visited Suzanne, who was blind from an overdose of medication and could speak only by mouthing her words.

One day she touched Cathy and mouthed, "You aren't going home to your husband, are you?"

"No, Mom."

"Does he know?"

"Yes."

Then Suzanne patted her daughter's hand and said, "That's all right, honey. I've done it two or three times myself."

That remains one of Cathy's only memories of hearing words of affirmation and acceptance from her mother. Ironically, it came after Cathy had tasted just a bit of the pain her mother had worked so long to protect her from. Suzanne died soon after, at the age of fifty-nine.

Cathy considers herself a carbon copy of her mother. But it has taken her years to resurrect the ravaged self-image that Suzanne tried to destroy. She never was allowed to just be herself, to behave the way she was designed to behave.

Now remarried, Cathy has two children of her own. A few years ago she visited her mother's best friend, Connie, and showed her Suzanne's grandchildren. As Cathy left, Connie began to cry. "This is so wonderful," she said. "You're doing such a great job with your kids.... You are everything your mother wanted you to be."

Those final words rang in Cathy's mind for the next several hours. "It sent chills down my spine," she recalls. "It shocked me to think I might actually be pleasing to my mother now."

### The Reflection in the Mirror

When your child looks in the mirror, what does she see? I'm not talking about the mirror on the wall. I mean the mirror of your eyes.

You may not be aware of it, but you are a mirror.

The other morning I was looking through different drawers, trying to find a mirror to examine the bald spot some crazy person said was developing on the back of my head. After I finally found the mirror under a pile of old electric curlers, combs, brushes, and bobby pins, I held it up and was momentarily startled. I had the mirror turned to the side that magnifies, so that my face, larger than life, jumped out at me.

With that side, I noticed far more facial blemishes and wrinkles than I did with the normal side (which I much preferred). It also made my normal features look distorted and repulsive. Fortunately, the convex side also provided no help in finding that "bald spot," so I can go on believing it does not exist.

That's the kind of mirror parents can be to their children—a mirror that exaggerates blemishes and turns nice-looking features into something ugly. This is what Suzanne reflected to Cathy. And since that's what Cathy saw, that's what she came to believe about herself.

In *The Art of Sensitive Parenting,* Katherine C. Kersey wrote: "Children come into the world not knowing who they are. They learn who they are from those around them."[1] You are a mirror your child looks into every day, and you reflect back to her what she will come to believe about herself. These reflections are like snapshots of herself that she pastes into an imaginary photo album, laying the foundation of her identity.

Initially, your child cannot see herself directly; she only sees herself through the eyes of the important people in her life. A person's self-image is usually based not on who she is, but on who she *thinks* she is. And a child thinks she is who her parents believe her to be.

As a parent, you have a choice of reflecting acceptance or rejection, approval or disapproval. To a great degree, whether or not your child feels wanted and worthwhile depends on what she sees in your "mirror."

## FAULTY MIRRORS

As you've studied your child's design, you've learned about many of the strengths inherent in her behavioral style. So what will you do with that knowledge?

I'm amazed at the number of parents who know what their children can do well but instead spend most of their time focusing on their kids' failures and weaknesses. Sometimes the parents don't know any better, and sometimes it's just a bad habit.

Another problem is that some parents believe too much praise can make a child weak and spoiled. As with many errant beliefs, this one contains some grains of truth. Parents should take responsibility for addressing their child's faults. And if a child receives an extreme amount of praise—hearing from her parents that she's always good, always right, and never wrong in her behavior—she could grow up spoiled, selfish, and amoral. She may never come to understand her sin nature and her capacity to do wrong.

Unfortunately, some Christian parents move to the other extreme: In their efforts to help their child deal with weakness, disobedience, and sin, they rarely affirm the child. There's no balance. The child sees only the bad reflected by her parents, never the good. So she grows up with a poor self-image, and believes she's destined for failure.

### "I Just Can't Keep Up with Him"

Lee is a high "D" child with an enormous supply of energy. He doesn't walk, he runs. He can't pass through a door frame without jumping up to touch the header. He's like a meteor that lights up the sky in the morning and doesn't burn itself out until several hours after bedtime. His parents, however, are more easygoing and reserved. Lee's mother is a high "S" and his father a high "C."

It seems he can never do anything right in their eyes. They always seem to yell at him for running too much or talking too loudly.

He wishes he could please his parents more, and he thinks they wish they'd had a different son, instead of him. Of course, they've never said anything like that to him, but that's how he interprets their reflection of his behavior. On numerous occasions, though, he has overheard his mom tell her friends, "I just don't know what we are going to do with that child. Go, go, go, go.... I can't keep up with him. This kid wears me out."

Since he knows that he is not like his parents, Lee secretly believes something is wrong with him. His inner design will not allow him to submit passively, so he takes his frustration out on other kids. By first grade he's become bossy and demanding on the playground. He always wants things done his way, and none of the kids likes to play with him.

When Lee's parents meet with his teacher, she tells them he plays too rough with other kids. She also tells them that Lee is rather stubborn and refuses to follow instructions. "When your son gets an idea in his head, you can't budge him. He has his own way of doing things and he won't listen to reason."

That night his parents tell Lee that he will be punished if he continues this behavior, which only makes Lee feel more worthless. And that makes him act even worse at school.

As a teenager, Lee learns to channel his aggression and frustration into football. He becomes a star linebacker; he loves to knock people down. By his senior year he attracts the attention of college scouts, and he wins a scholarship to a top school.

Lee is pleased that his parents come to his games, but he still feels he rarely pleases them. His father always asks him about his grades, and wishes he would read more books.

Lee feels like a success in at least one area of life, but eventually he will face a tough fork in the road. At some point his athletic career will come to an end, either from injury, or graduation, or age. And when it does, and the cheering stops, he'll still be left with those old reflections in his mind, the images he saw in his parents eyes. And the old voices will return, telling him that he's worthless.

The sad thing about Lee, and hundreds like him, is that he perceived that something was wrong with the "real" person inside. Because of parental pressure and expectations, this person inside never had a chance to fully develop. He felt unloved and unacceptable for who he really was. By not valuing his strengths, his parents pushed him further into the negative aspects of his style. Early on, he tried to be what they wanted. But this was impossible, because in trying to stuff who he was, the negative sides of his behavior kept popping up, creating more antagonism toward others and anxiety for himself.

Fortunately, some kids like Lee are able to cast off the mask. But for others, the wrestling match between the real self and the "fabricated" self may last a lifetime.

## THE POWER OF A PARENT'S WORDS

Our prisons, courts, and hospitals deal every day with people who are paying the price of warped mirrors. I once heard about a baseball player who spoke to a group of prisoners. He related the story of how he pitched every day after school with his dad. When he would throw the ball over his dad's head, his father would say, "Son, some day you are going to be a major league pitcher."

On another occasion, he threw a wild pitch and broke a window. His father said, "Son, with an arm like that, you'll be in the big leagues someday." The pitcher told the prisoners, "All that I am I attribute to my father who believed I could be something."

After he spoke, a prisoner came up to thank him for the message. He said, "My father did the same thing as your father, but he constantly told me, 'Son, one day you are going to wind up in prison.' I guess I fulfilled his expectations."

Parental disapproval usually leads to long-term emotional and psychological difficulties. In fact, history books are filled with examples of the brutal impact such people have had on the course of human events.

But there can be a positive impact as well. In their excellent book, *How to Talk So Kids Will Listen and Listen So Kids Will Talk,* Adel Faber and Elaine Mazlish relate the following story that happened after one of their workshops.

One day, toward the end of a session on roles, a father started us reminiscing. He said, "I remember when I was a kid, I used to come to my dad with all kinds of crazy schemes. He'd always listen to me very seriously. Then he'd say, 'Son, you may have your head in the clouds, but your feet are rooted in the ground.' Now that picture he gave me of myself—as someone who dreams, but also someone who knows how to deal with reality—has been one that's helped me through some pretty rough times.... I was wondering whether anyone else here had that kind of experience."

There was a thoughtful silence as each of us began to reach into the past to look for the message that had marked our lives. Slowly, together, we began to remember aloud:

"When I was a little boy, my grandmother always used to tell me I had wonderful hands. Whenever I'd thread a needle for her or untie the knots in her wool, she'd say I had 'goldeneh hendt' [golden hands]. I think it's one of the reasons I decided to become a dentist."

"My first year of teaching was overwhelming for me. I used to tremble whenever my chairman dropped in to observe a lesson. Afterwards, he'd give me one or two pointers, but then he'd always add, 'I never worry about you, Ellen. Basically, you're self-correcting.' I wonder if he ever knew what an inspiration those words were to me. I hung onto them every day. They helped me believe in myself...."

Almost everyone in the group had a memory to share. When the session ended, we just sat there and looked at each other. The father who had started us all remembering shook his head in wonderment. When he spoke, he spoke for us all. "Never underestimate the power of your words upon a young person's life!"[2]

What are you reflecting to your child? What does she see in your eyes when you talk with her—or discipline her? Your mirror not only influences her self-esteem, but also her behavior. If you can reflect positive images to your child, you can have a profound impact upon whom she becomes.

In the next three chapters I will show you several practical steps you can take to reflect these positive images to your child. I believe you'll find these parenting principles some of the most practical you'll ever read.

## NOTES

1. Katherine C. Kersey, *The Art of Sensitive Parenting* (Herndon, Va.: Acropolis Books, 1983).

2. Adel Faber and Elaine Mazlish, *How to Talk So Kids Will Listen and Listen So Kids Will Talk* (New York: Avon Books, 1980), 224-225.

CHAPTER ELEVEN

# MIRRORING YOUR CHILD'S STRENGTHS... AND WEAKNESSES

Bronson Alcott may not have been the best provider for his family. He was a philosopher and a dreamer. But he knew how to reach the hearts of his daughters and let them know how special they were.

Recently I found a remarkable letter he wrote to his daughters, Abba, Louisa, and Elizabeth. It was written in 1842, in that age before phone calls replaced letter writing as the primary form of long-distance communication. I've edited the letter slightly to make it easier to read. As you go through it, note the way this father affirms his children:

> My dear girls:
>
> I think of you all every day and desire to see you all again: Abba with her beauty-loving eyes and sweet visions of graceful motions, of golden hues and all fair and mystic shows and shapes...
>
> Louisa with her quick and ready service, her agile limbs and boundless curiosity, her penetrating mind and tear-shedding heart, alive to all moving, breathing things...
>
> Elizabeth with her quiet-loving disposition and serene thoughts, her happy gentleness, deep sentiment...and mother too, whose unsleeping love and painstaking hands provide for your comforts and pleasant things and is your hope and stay and now more near and important to you while I am taken from your eyes.
>
> All and each of you I have in my mind: daily I see you in my thoughts and as I lay my head on my pillow at night or wake from sleep in the morning...nor can the tumbling waters hide

> my group of loves from my eyes: the little cottage there behind the Elm, the garden round, strawberry red or coloured vines...or corn barn play house, or street or bridge or winding stream, or Anna or Louisa, their lessons loved (and learned by heart, not rote) and Lizzie too with little Ab in parlor, study, chamber, lawn, with needle, book or pen...
>
> And so you see, my gentle girls, I cannot leave you quite: though my body is far away my mind is near and all the while, I hear and see and touch and think and feel your very selves—the life that lives in all you are and say and do, the mind, the Heart, the Soul—the God that dwells in you. And now be loving little girls and grow far more fair with every day and when I come to see my garden plot then shall my flowers scent the fields and I shall joy in every scent they lend, in every tint and form they wear. So now, my dears, adieu.
>
> Let mother read this with you and talk long and sweetly with her about what is in it and then kiss her all and each other and then her all again for Father's sake.[1]

This was a father who understood how to encourage his daughters. He didn't just praise his daughters. He used descriptive phrases to help picture their strengths:

"Abba with her beauty-loving eyes and sweet visions of graceful motions...."

"Louisa with her quick and ready service, her agile limbs and boundless curiosity...."

"Elizabeth with her quiet-loving disposition and serene thoughts, her happy gentleness, deep sentiment...."

I suspect that at least one of these girls inherited some of her father's ability to dream, because years later Louisa May Alcott made her family the model for her best-selling book *Little Women.*

### THE VALUE OF DESCRIPTIVE PRAISE

I'd like to add a new phrase to your vocabulary: "descriptive praise." This is the technique Bronson Alcott used in his letter, and it's a tool I've found extremely helpful in reflecting strengths to my kids. It's the first practical step you can take to be a positive mirror to your child.

Descriptive praise is a special type of praise. Remember, the function of a mirror is to reflect an image as it is. That's what descriptive praise does. It reflects a child's behavior in a way that causes him to feel loved and capable, and it teaches him to feel good about the things he's done.

With descriptive praise, you concentrate more on *who the person is*, his behavioral traits, rather than on *what he does*. Over the long haul, if a child receives praise primarily for what he does, he grows up basing his self-worth on his performance and how well he measures up to what is expected of him. In *Bringing Up Kids Without Tearing Them Down*, Kevin Leman wrote, "Many people—adults and children—believe that, 'Unless I perform, unless I achieve, unless I do things people like, I won't be loved or approved of. I'll be a nothing.' "[2]

Let's say your child takes the initiative to clean all the bathrooms in the house. Rather than merely saying "Great job!" use descriptive praise: "Dan, I noticed that you cleaned all the bathrooms without being asked. Mom and I really appreciate that—it saves us a lot of work. And the fact that you did it shows you have the ability to take initiative."

The difference is subtle but important. By describing his behavior and character, you let your child know that he has self-worth because of the unique way God designed him. This kind of praise helps a child know himself and feel good about the natural strengths God has given him.

### THREE STEPS TO DESCRIPTIVE PRAISE

To begin using descriptive praise to encourage your child, I suggest three steps:

1. *Describe what you see.* "Nicole, I've noticed that you work very hard to keep your room neat and tidy."

2. *If possible, describe how you feel.* "It's a pleasure to walk into this room."

3. *Sum up the positive strength in one or two words.* "That's what I call being responsible."[3]

The first step helps the child picture his behavior. The room is neat and tidy. The homework was finished without the parent having to tell the child to do it. The child has colored a pretty picture for you.

The second step helps him see how his behavior can benefit and please other people. "I appreciate how you have cleaned up your room." "It is a big help to me when you finish your homework without my having to tell you. Thanks!" "It makes me feel so good inside to know that you colored this picture just for me!"

And assigning a descriptive term to your child's behavior helps to reinforce it. The idea is to tell the child something about himself that he may not have known before, to give him a verbal snapshot of himself.

Used consistently, descriptive praise may be the best practical way to train your child according to his design. It shows a child what his strengths are and how to use them constructively. For example:

"Daniel, I noticed today that when the other boys began to make fun of Joseph, you stood up for him. I know that made him feel like you are his friend. It took courage to stand up to those other boys." (Or, "That's what I call being a loyal friend.")

"Courtney, I can see that doing things just right is very important to you. You really worked hard on your science project, trying to get every detail in place. That's what I call *excellence.*"

"Kyle, I can tell that you make up your mind quickly and like others to do things your way. That helps us get things done in our house. That's called being *decisive.*"

"Jason, I see that you sorted out all of the pencils, markers, and crayons and put them in separate boxes. Thanks for your help! You are very *organized.*"

### How to Begin Using Descriptive Praise

To your child, descriptive praise can be a source of lifelong encouragement. If you're serious about reflecting positive strengths, I have five suggestions:

*First, use "one liners" and "one-minute praises" to affirm your child.* Throughout the day, I look for opportunities to describe behavioral strengths I can reinforce in my children. Often I make brief one-liner comments, such as, "You have a lot of drive," or, "You always try to do your best work." Note the section at the end of this chapter containing more one-liners you can use with your child.

Then look for opportunities to expand one-liners into one-minute praises. Become familiar with different behavioral traits to watch for. In Appendix A you will find a very useful tool: "Forty Behavioral Strengths You Can Mirror to Your Child." I've listed ten strengths for each of the four primary behavioral styles. By spending more time describing what you see in your child and seeing the behavior as a strength, your child will come to specifically understand how God uniquely designed him.

A friend of mine, Merry, has observed that her eleven-year-old "S" daughter, Bethany, sometimes displays a special compassion for others. On one occasion, she attended the funeral of her friend's grandmother and made a special effort to be with her friend and hold her hand during the service. On another day, at the roller rink, Bethany noticed several girls laughing at someone who couldn't skate well. Bethany rolled over to the girl, helped her up, and skated around the floor with her the rest of the afternoon.

Merry wants to encourage Bethany to continue showing compassion for others, so she went out of her way to do a one-minute praise with her at bedtime: "Bethany, I noticed that you made a special effort to be with Kelly at the funeral. That's what I call compassion. That means you have the ability to be sensitive to the hurts of other people because you have an understanding heart. You'll go out of your way to help a person because you understand how she feels. Compassionate people like you are the kind of people others like to have for a friend."

*Second, let your child overhear you tell others about his strengths.* When Papa and Grandma came for a visit, I told them that Callie was the one person in our family who didn't mind going up to the waiter or waitress in restaurants and asking for whatever we needed. When I said, "Callie has the strength of being assertive, and that means she will easily do what some people feel uncomfortable doing," Callie's face beamed with delight. Grandma was impressed, and Callie saw that her behavior, which was a natural strength for her, was a valuable asset.

*Third, draw attention to those times when your child acts out of character.* Just because some behaviors do not come as naturally for your child as others doesn't mean he cannot make a special effort to learn those skills. This is a function of growth and maturity. A mature person knows his strengths and develops skills to compensate for his limitations.

When your "D" child demonstrates sensitivity, when your "I" child pays attention to key details, when your "S" child moves boldly into unknown territory, or when your "C" child takes a risk, make sure to notice and tell him about it. In so doing, he will learn to become more flexible and balanced.

My son, Chad, does not normally pay attention to details. On one occasion, when his mother asked him to run into the grocery store and buy a can of peas, he did something that surprised all of us. He figured out that the brand of peas we normally buy and which were on sale were more expensive than some other brand of peas. Then he took the initiative to buy the cheaper peas.

Karen said, "You figured out that the cans of peas on sale—the three-for-a-dollar ones—were actually more expensive than the brand that wasn't on sale. That's what I call paying *attention to details.* Thanks for saving us money."

*Fourth, write your child special notes and letters.* Kids seem to love personal, hand-written notes—perhaps because the written words serve as a tangible reminder of your love and of their strengths. Many people save encouraging letters and notes and reread them many times.

I like using Post-It™ notes. You can put them up on the bathroom mirror, in lunch boxes, or on the night stand in your child's bedroom.

One evening, Kristi (my high "C/S" child) invited me into her room.

She said, "Dad, look around. What do you think?" I replied, "Kristi, as I look around your room I can see that everything has a place and everything is in it's place. That's what I call *organization.* I'm impressed. This is a big help to your mother and me."

Later I followed up with a note: "Dear Kristi, I can see that you give a lot of time and energy to making sure things in your room are in their place. You are an organized person. Thanks for your help! Love, Dad."

Callie, our "S/D" child, is shy about some things, but when there is a task to be done, she volunteers right away. We discovered this when we were eating at a local restaurant. We had finished our basket of wheat rolls, and I asked both Chad and Kristi to ask the waiter for more. They were too embarrassed to approach a stranger, but Callie immediately volunteered.

The next day I wrote a note to Callie. Karen had to read it to her, but it drove the point home anyway: "Dear Callie, I noticed that you like to volunteer for things other people sometimes don't want to do. That's what I call being assertive. That means you easily take action even when other people are hesitant or looking for an easy way out. Your willingness to get the bread last night was a help to us all. Thanks! Love, Dad."

*Finally, give your child the opportunity to take on responsibilities which utilize his strengths.* On a recent vacation to Florida, I asked Kristi to be in charge of keeping our van organized. She thought that was a great idea. I let everyone know that they needed to follow her instructions, and we all made an effort to compliment her for her organizational skills.

Last summer I gave Chad the responsibility for mowing our lawn. This has played well with his "D" style, because it gives him the chance to be in control of something. He even decides when the lawn needs to be mowed. And it takes one more chore off my back!

His creative side also comes through. The other day I came home to find that he had mowed "FSU" in large letters on the back yard. He had mowed the lawn and then come back and lowered the blades one notch. The initials of Florida State University, my alma mater, were only visible from the second floor of our home. I praised Chad's creativity, but this time I told him that once was enough!

### MIRRORING YOUR CHILD'S WEAKNESSES

No matter how hard you work on encouraging your child by mirroring his strengths, you can't avoid the fact that he also has limitations—blind spots or weaknesses which trouble you. You probably confront these weaknesses every day!

As you address these weaknesses, however, you have a choice: Will you do it in an *encouraging* or a *discouraging* manner? Do you want to build your child's self-esteem or tear it down?

Consider the following remarks from parents to their children:

"What am I going to do with you? Don't you want to get involved in something and make something of yourself?"

"Look at this room. You need to clean up this mess. How can you live in such a pigsty?"

"If you're going to do a job, do it right the first time."

"This is good work. Now next time it can be even better if you would...."

In each case, the parent has mixed two messages into one: While trying to correct the child's behavior, the parent also is telling the child, "I'm not satisfied with you. You need to be different."

Ironically, many children resort to bad behavior to gain their parents' attention and approval. Usually, the worse a child's behavior, the greater his need for approval. The more rebellious or withdrawn he becomes, the more he needs to see reflections of love and acceptance.

The problem is that his behavior is self-defeating. He deeply craves approval, but his inappropriate behavior makes that next to impossible. So he goes round and round, digging his own personal dungeon.

Now, all parents lose their cool sometimes! Occasional negative blasts are not permanently damaging, especially if you admit when you are wrong and ask for forgiveness. But a child who receives constant negative or critical reflections will conclude, "I guess I am a lousy person. If my own parents don't like me, who could?"

Strengths are to be affirmed, but certain behaviors must also be limited. We need to make sure the image we reflect back to a child is affirming of his inner design. Here are a couple of suggestions:

*1. Regard your child's weaknesses as strengths pushed to an extreme.* Every strength, when pushed to an extreme or used inappropriately, can become a limitation. As your child discovers his bent, he also needs to learn that every strength has a flip-side limitation which must be kept in check.

The following chart shows how different behavioral strengths of each style can easily lead to weaknesses ("Forty Behavioral Strengths" in Appendix A also provides related weaknesses):

| | Strength | Corresponding Limitation |
|---|---|---|
| **D** | Goal-oriented | Impatient |
| | Confident | Self-sufficient |
| | Competitive | Attacks first |
| | Determined | Stubborn |
| | Courageous | Reckless |
| | Direct, straightforward | Blunt, tactless |
| **I** | Enthusiastic | Excitable, emotional |
| | Good communicator | Talks too much |
| | Optimistic | Unrealistic |
| | Imaginative | Day dreamer |
| | People-person | Disorganized with tasks and things |
| | Spontaneous | Impulsive, undisciplined |
| **S** | Stable | Lacks enthusiasm |
| | Steady | Resists change |
| | Easygoing | Indecisive |
| | Agreeable | Over accommodating |
| | Soft-hearted | Easily manipulated |
| | Helpful | Smothering |
| **C** | Analytical | Nit-picking |
| | Cautious | Unsociable, suspicious |
| | Conscientious | Worries too much |
| | High personal standards | Judgmental, critical |
| | Strives for excellence | Perfectionistic |
| | Intuitive, sensitive | Easily hurt by criticism |

2. *Address the weakness while also affirming the strength.* Show your child how the strength, when taken to an extreme, can hurt or offend other people or create problems for him. Rather than being helpful, the strength can become hurtful.

"Blake ['D'], I can see that you really play hard in order to win. That's known as being a *competitive* person. *One thing you will want to remember* is that sometimes, a competitive person can attack people and be overly aggressive in situations that are not supposed to be competitive."

"Liz ['I'], I can tell you really like people and you want them to like you. *One thing to keep in mind* is, sometimes that can lead you away from doing what you know is right."

"Sam ['S'], it's easy to see that you go out of your way to get along with people. *There are times when* giving in may allow others to take advantage of you."

"Katlin ['C'], I know you consider everything you do very carefully. *Sometimes, when that strength is pushed out of balance,* others may feel like you care more about your work than them."

When correcting behavior in this way, it's important not to use the words "but" or "however," as in, "Jeff, you have very high standards, *but* that can also make others feel like they don't measure up to you." If you affirm a strength and then use "but," you will negate the strength.

Use phrases such as "One thing you need to remember" or "One thing to keep in mind" or "Sometimes that strength can become a weakness." This teaches your child the relationship between the strength and the weakness, without negating the strength.

## KIDS UNDERSTAND MORE THAN WE THINK

A few years ago, Chad ("D") got into a big argument with Karen at breakfast. He was dawdling and not getting ready in time to catch his ride to school. As Karen got more and more frustrated, trying to motivate him to get his things together, Chad shot back with some comments that were disrespectful.

Karen became very directive and told him that he would have to stay inside after school for the way he had spoken to her. That's what she needed to do. In the heat of conflict, usually the parent must use a more directive style in order to bring the conflict under control. The more emotional the child, the less you will be able to reason with him. Logic will not overpower emotion.

I overheard Karen and Chad's discussion from the bathroom, and even though Karen had disciplined Chad, I wanted to discuss this with him later. I felt I needed to discuss his behavior at a less emotionally charged time.

That night Chad and I lay in his bed, and I brought up the conflict from earlier in the day. I wanted him to understand that the reason he was disciplined so often was because of his insensitivity, which was an overextension of a positive strength God has given him.

I said, "You know, one of the great strengths that God has given you is that you say exactly what you think. That's called being *direct* with people. That can be helpful to others because they never have to wonder where they stand with you; you'll tell them.

"One thing you need to remember is that every strength can be used in a way that is hurtful, rather than helpful. When you say exactly what you think to your mother or me—or any adult for that matter—it can come across as being disrespectful. Or if you say exactly what you think to your friends, they may think you are just being mean."

I wondered whether he was taking this in, so I asked, "Do you understand what I'm saying about strengths and weaknesses?'

"I think so," he replied.

"Well, explain it to me so I will understand what you're hearing."

Then Chad said, "It's kind of like dry ice."

"Dry ice?" I thought to myself, *Good grief, where's he headed with this?*

"Yeah, dry ice," Chad said. "It's really good because it keeps things really cold. But if you take it out and hold it in your hand, it will burn you."

Whoah!

Dry ice...he made the connection. That illustration has formed the basis for many other discussions about strengths and weaknesses. In each case, Chad clearly sees the need to change his behavior, but at the same time he feels encouraged because he understands why he acts the way he does. I'm not telling him to quit being himself and be like someone else. I'm training him to keep his natural strengths in balance.

In the next chapter I'll look at another aspect of the "reflection principle": reflecting a child's emotions.

## ONE-LINERS YOU CAN USE TO REFLECT YOUR CHILD'S STRENGTHS

### FOR "D" CHILDREN:

You are a determined person.
You have confidence in yourself.
You have strong ideas about things.
You aren't easily sidetracked.
You can't be pushed to do something you don't want to do.
You say exactly what you think.
You set your mind on something and go after it with everything you have.
You feel able to handle things on your own.
You really stick to things that interest you.
You are committed and decisive.
You are assertive.
You are independent and capable.

You charge into new situations without fear.
You are quick to respond to a situation and seek a solution.
You know what you want and you go after it.
You really play hard to win.
You can make a decision without consulting others.
You have a very honest way of expressing exactly what you think about things.
You like to get results when you do things.
You have a lot of drive.
You have a strong will.
You are up front with people.
You need time to do something physical to recharge.

**FOR "I" CHILDREN:**

You are an outgoing person.
You have a lot of enthusiasm. It's contagious.
You want to have positive relationships with others.
You have a wonderful sense of humor.
You notice everything going on around you.
You are eager to participate in everything that is going on.
You have such a creative imagination.
You want to be liked by other people.
You are really flexible.
You are full of surprises.
You are full of energy.
You need to wiggle and move.
You really like people and want them to like you.
You really enjoy being with people.
You make others feel comfortable.
You seem to look for the best in people and situations.
You don't seem bothered by loose ends and details.
You have a happy spirit about you.
You are fun to be with.
You have a way with words.
You share your thoughts and feelings easily.
You have a unique ability to motivate people.
You are a great storyteller.
You are very gifted at expressing your thoughts, opinions, and feelings.
Words seem to come easily for you.
You are a persuasive person.
Being around people seems to recharge your batteries.

**FOR "S" CHILDREN:**

You form deep and lasting relationships.
You are a caring person.
You are an accepting person.
You can feel other people's hurts and stress.
You like to watch before participating.
You like to check things out before you jump in.
You need to know what to expect.
Change is difficult for you. That's okay.
You are easy to talk to.
You like to know how something is done. You like things explained step by step.
You don't rush into decisions.
You like things to stay the same.
You stick to things you know work well.
You take your time to do things step by step.
You seem to go out of your way to get along with everyone.
You are a good listener.
You have a compassionate nature and a tender heart.
You always follow through.
You seem to be a sensitive person.
You don't seem to like conflicts or making waves.
You come across as being quite easygoing.
You have a calming influence on other people.
You don't seem pressured by time.
You are a trusting type of person.
You like to give people the benefit of the doubt.
You need time to yourself to recharge.

**FOR "C" CHILDREN:**

You tend to be a quiet person.
You have high standards.
You always try to do your best work.
You are attentive to what others say and feel.
You like things to be organized.
You do things precisely and accurately.
You want to understand all you can about what you are planning to do.
You like things done in a logical way.
You seem to weigh things out carefully.
You are a good evaluator.
You like to think about things and then decide.

You are a serious person. That doesn't mean you are unhappy.
You think deeply about things.
You like things to be "just right."
You have a questioning mind.
You are finely tuned into the things around you.
You are interested in key details.
You enjoy spending time by yourself.
You need quiet time to recharge.

## NOTES

1. Alexandra Towle, ed., *Fathers* (New York: Simon and Schuster, Watermark Press, 1986), 36-37.

2. Kevin Leman, *Bringing Up Kids Without Tearing Them Down* (New York: Delacorte Press, 1993), 169. Dr. Leman's chapter entitled "The Crucial Difference Between Praise and Encouragement" echoes the principles I share here. He prefers to use the term "encouragement." I have chosen the term "descriptive praise."

3. Adele Faber and Elaine Mazlish, *How to Talk So Kids Will Listen and Listen So Kids Will Talk* (New York: Avon Books, 1980), 186.

CHAPTER TWELVE

# MIRRORING YOUR CHILD'S EMOTIONS

Anna usually brings excellent report cards home from school. But one day she arrives home with a look of disappointment and sadness. Reluctantly she hands her mother the latest report card.

*Mom:* "What's the matter, Anna?"

*Anna:* "It's not good."

*Mom:* "Let's see.... Anna, I don't see what the problem is. This is a wonderful report card!"

*Anna:* "It is not. I got a B in science."

*Mom:* "But you got an A in History, an A in Math, an A in English, and an A in Spanish. You're doing great in all your subjects. There's no reason for you to be upset about this."

*Anna:* "Mom, I only got a B in science, and I even did an extra credit project."

*Mom:* "Maybe your science teacher is just harder than your other teachers. You're blowing this all out of proportion."

Does this story sound at all familiar? It should, because all too often we try to talk our children out of feeling the way they do. It would be comical, if it weren't so tragic.

*Child:* "Mom, I'm tired."

*Mom:* "You couldn't possibly be tired. You went to bed early last night and didn't get out of bed until 9:00 A.M."

*Child:* "But I *am* tired."

*Mom:* "You are *not!* Now hurry up and get your things together. We have to leave."

*Child*(crying): "I AM TIRED *and* I DON'T WANT TO GO!"

When a child falls and skins her knee, we know what to do: Clean the scrape and cover it with a bandage. But it's much more difficult when a child comes to us with emotional hurts.

We try to talk our children out of their feelings with logic, reasoning, and denial. These responses make our children feel like they are not being heard. When they feel misunderstood, they can transfer their anger or hurt to us. Could this be what Paul was referring to when he exhorted parents not to provoke their children to wrath (Ephesians 6:4)?

*Child:* "I hate Jason. Ever since he came into our family I don't have any fun anymore."

*Dad:* "That's a terrible thing to say about your little brother. You shouldn't say things like that. You know you don't mean it."

*Child:* "I do hate him. I wish he'd never been born."

*Dad:* "I don't want to hear you say anything like that again, young lady. Do you understand me? Do you?... Answer me!"

*Child:* "Yes!" (Stalks out of the room, holding in her anger.)

In all these examples, the parent attempts to contradict how the child feels with denial and reason. The parent wants to fix the problem and in the process denies the child's feelings.

Our whole approach to handling our children's emotions needs work. Many people grow up without any training in how to handle and express their emotions.

When your child looks at the mirror of your eyes, she needs to see an honest reflection of her emotions. This is the first step in showing her how to work through those emotions—and it's the step that too many parents leave out.

## EMOTIONS ARE PART OF LIFE

I feel a little silly stating something so obvious, but it's necessary: We can't help feeling emotions! They are part of us. The problem is that many of us don't know *what to do* with these emotions.

Sometimes we're happy, sometimes we aren't. Sometimes we're confused about how we feel. Sometimes we say things we don't really mean. Sometimes we may feel a certain way and it may not be logical.

When an emotionally mature person experiences a negative emotion, at some point she is able to go back and think through what made her feel that way. Then she will decide upon some steps she can take to improve her attitude or her situation.

If she becomes angry at her child, she will later ask herself questions such as: *Why was I so angry? Was he wrong? Was I wrong? What could I have done differently?* She will come to some conclusions and take steps to act differently in the future.

But let's say that while she is feeling the intense anger, she talks with a close friend who says, "You shouldn't feel this way. You're the one who's mostly at fault in the first place!"

That kind of statement will only intensify her anger. She becomes angry not only at her child, but also at the friend who doesn't understand her. She doesn't want to hear logic—in fact, she can't hear logic because her emotions are clouding her mind. She'll lash out at her friend, and she'll take longer to reach the point at which she can begin thinking clearly again.

That's what happens with many children. Many parents tell their children, either directly or indirectly, that certain emotions are not acceptable. When they are afraid, they're told there is nothing to be afraid of. When they hurt themselves and cry, they're told, "Be brave and dry up those tears," or "That little scratch can't hurt that much."

Feeling misunderstood is one of life's most discouraging emotions. The words of an anonymous poet tragically describe what may be a typical family:

*Two people who know they do not understand each other,*
*Breeding children whom they don't understand*
*And who will never understand them.*

Sad, but true. When you share your feelings, you want to be heard with understanding. You want someone to accept how you feel without judging you. You want some time to process your emotions before you sit down to logically work out a solution. But many times parents respond to their children's feelings in the opposite way from how they would want to be treated in similar circumstances. If you are going to "do unto your children as you would have others do unto you," you need to have a plan that will allow you to treat your children's feelings the way you would want to be treated in a similar situation.

## ARE YOU APATHETIC, SYMPATHETIC, OR EMPATHETIC?

To help your child deal with her emotions, it's important for you to develop the ability to show *empathy.* Empathy is listening with your heart as well as your head. When you show empathy, you let your child know you understand what she's feeling.

Perhaps a good way to understand empathy is to see it on a continuum.[1]

| Apathy | Empathy | Sympathy |
|---|---|---|
| I don't care. | Sounds like you are really afraid of leaving your friends. | Oh, I am so sorry. You poor thing. |

*Apathy* is defined as a "lack of emotional responsiveness or a lack of interest or concern." When I am apathetic, I am uninvolved. Parents can be so busy with their concerns that they send messages that their children interpret as, "I don't care."

When your child expresses her feelings and receives little or no response—when there is a quick, cliché-type answer, such as, "I'm sure it will all work out. Now go back outside and play"—she thinks, "My parents don't care. They don't love me."

On the opposite end of the spectrum is sympathy. Sympathy is defined as "feeling for" another person. When I sympathize, I become overinvolved in the other person's emotions. I respond in a gushy way that can come across as condescending. People don't want to be pitied; they want to be understood.

Listening *empathetically* means "feeling with" another person, yet remaining separate. This is what Paul refers to in Romans 12:15 when he said to, "Rejoice with those who rejoice; mourn with those who mourn." The empathetic person feels another person's hurt, but is not crippled by it. She is able to sense the other person's hurt, fear, disappointment, irritation, or frustration as if it were her own, but she remains detached enough to be a help and encouragement.

For example, when your...

- high "D" child is impatient and angry;
- your high "I" child is hurt because she was left off someone's party invitation list;
- your high "S" child worries about her first day at a new school;
- or your high "C" child seems overly concerned with missing a note in her clarinet solo in the school band concert.

...how do you respond? Here are some possibilities:

*Denial:* "You're upset over nothing. Now just forget it and move on."

*Optimism:* "Look on the bright side."

*Advice:* "You know what I think you should do?"

*Blaming:* "Are you sure this isn't your fault? What did you do to cause this?"

*Pity:* "Oh, you poor thing. I feel so sorry for you."

*Lecture:* "This wouldn't have happened if you had..."

*Empathy:* "Boy, I can see you are ___________ (angry, irritated, bothered, hurt, embarrassed, sad, afraid, fearful, upset, concerned, worried, disappointed). I think I would feel the same way if that had happened to me."[3]

Be aware that your behavioral style may hinder your ability to empathize with your child. The *Directive* parent, for instance, tends to give a quick, direct command in an attempt to fix the situation and the person. This parent may have a hard time identifying with an "I" child's need to be accepted by her peer group.

The *Interactive* parent often dismisses the child's concern by optimistically saying, "Hey, lighten up. Don't worry, it's all going to work out all right." Since she is not detail-oriented, she probably will have difficulty understanding a "C" child's inner turmoil when things don't turn out just right. The quick-fix answer of both the "D" and "I" parents may seem like apathy to a child.

The *Supportive* parent has the most natural ability to empathize but may carry that ability too far and offer sympathy instead. She may lose the ability to separate her feelings from those of the other person. At the same time, she may not be able to understand how a "D" child can become so angry so quickly. The patient "S" parent cannot identify with such impatience.

The *Corrective* parent may have trouble holding back advice or overanalyzing every situation in order to correct the child's problems for her. Again, this can come across as cold and sterile. The cautious nature of the "C" parent (which can be expressed as pessimism) can't identify with the positive emotions of her "I" child who takes everything in stride.

Some of you may have an easier time demonstrating empathy to your child. But empathy is a skill that can be learned. I have three simple steps to help you.

### STEP ONE: LISTEN!

When you are sad, angry, depressed, or confused, sometimes all you need is a listening ear. You want someone who will listen to you express your problem without giving any advice or reflecting disapproval or judgment.

Allow your child to express her feelings to you without judgment. Resist giving the answers to her problem. Often, that's all she needs—the knowledge that you care enough to take time to listen.

Have her tell you everything that happened. You may need to ask questions to draw her out: What happened? What did you say? How did that make you feel? Be careful, though, to not let this come across as interrogation.

### STEP TWO: ACCEPT AND REFLECT HER FEELINGS WITHOUT JUDGMENT.

Again, do this by serving as a mirror—not just of her strengths, but of her emotions as well. This is another way you train up your child according to her bent. Each style has a characteristic emotional makeup that tends to be consistent, and we need to understand how who we are affects how we feel.

Acknowledge the emotions you see in your child, without evaluation or distortion. Describe the feeling you see.

"Boy, you are really *angry* about losing the game."

"It sounds like you are really *frustrated* with your friends."

It's also important to describe the right degree of emotion. You can communicate the intensity of the feeling by adding adverbs.

"You feel a *little* sad because your friends didn't invite you."

"You feel *quite* sad because your friends left you out."

"You feel *very* sad that your friends didn't include you."

"You feel *deeply* sad because your friends didn't invite you."

Haim G. Ginott points out that these reflective responses help children (and adults for that matter) become aware of their inner world of emotions:

> How can we help a child to know his feelings? We can do so by serving as a mirror to his emotions. A child learns about his physical likeness by seeing his image in a mirror. He learns about his emotional likeness by hearing his feelings reflected by us....
>
> The function of an emotional mirror is to reflect feeling as they are, without distortion:
>
> "It looks as though you are very angry."
>
> "It sounds like you hate him very much."
>
> "It seems that you are disgusted with the whole setup."
>
> To a child who has such feelings, these statements are most helpful. They show him clearly what his feelings are. Clarity of image, whether a looking glass or in an emotional mirror, provides opportunity for self-initiated grooming and change."[3]

When you acknowledge your child's feelings, do not parrot her words verbatim. If you do, she will catch on to what you are doing and doubt your sincerity.

Repeating and rephrasing may be the best way to draw out your child without putting her on the defensive. By putting her feelings into words, you help her better understand how she feels.

We can also give our children's emotions a name. When Callie's friends left her out of a new club they formed, I said, "I bet you are angry and disappointed." When classmates teased Jared about his new braces, his mother said, "You must have been embarrassed."

Giving a name to your children's feelings is a way to reflect back to them, so they learn that their emotions are normal and acceptable. It also helps let them know we understand what they are feeling. This step may be all that's needed to help a child deal with her emotions.

Recently I was in a home and heard a couple of family members teasing a ten-year-old boy about a girl he knew at school. Later, his sister came downstairs and reported that the boy was crying because his feelings were hurt.

The father could have laughed it off and said, "Well, that's what happens with kids—they need to learn how to deal with the opposite sex!" He could have told his son, "There's nothing to be hurt about—they were just having fun. You need to learn to take a joke."

But this father was able to understand what his son was feeling. Boys that age are just developing an interest in girls, and they feel awkward and even frightened around them. So the dad went upstairs and found his son sobbing on the bed.

"It really hurts when people make fun of you, doesn't it?" the dad asked.

"Yeah, they know I don't liked to be picked on, especially about girls," replied the son.

"It was embarrassing for you, wasn't it? I don't like it when people do that to me, either."

And with that, the tears began to dry up. The boy knew his dad understood how he felt, and that made him feel better.

### STEP THREE: IF NECESSARY, "REVISIT" THE EMOTION LATER AND TALK ABOUT IT.

In many cases you won't need to take this step. But with big problems or after displays of extreme emotion, you'll want to talk with your child about the issue at a later time. Do it after the feelings have died down and the child's head is clear. She'll be more receptive to the discussion then.

This is when you can reason with her, point her to Scripture, and seek to learn what is causing her problem. Ask questions like these:

"What did you learn from the experience?"

"How could you handle things differently next time?"

"What do you think about your attitude?"
"Do you need to ask forgiveness of anyone?"
"What can the Lord teach you through this?"

## DOWN IN THE MOUTH

As I thought through this section, I couldn't help but remember how God dealt with one of his children in a similar way. When God asked Jonah to go to Nineveh, Jonah wanted no part of it. In fact, he caught a ship headed out in the opposite direction from Nineveh and hid himself in the hold of the ship.

I think Jonah may have been a core "C." God gave him what he needed—private time to process his fear and emotional turmoil. Jonah's "voyage to the bottom of the sea" in the belly of a great fish gave him time to reconsider God's invitation to confront the Ninevites and call for their repentance.

With his amphibious landing on the beach, Jonah hit the ground running and delivered the message word-perfect. "Forty more days and Nineveh will be destroyed."

It must have been a shock to Jonah that the people of this wicked city listened to his message and humbled themselves in repentance before God. When God saw that they had turned from their evil ways, He didn't destroy them.

So all's well that ends well, right? No. Justice was not served. They got off too easily, at least as far as Jonah was concerned. The text says, "Jonah was greatly displeased and became angry" (Jonah 4:1).

More time alone. Out to the countryside he went to sit and stew about it. He became so depressed that he asked God to take his life.

God asked one question, "Have you any right to be angry?" That was it. No lecture, no sermon. He allowed Jonah time to process his emotional condition and the question.

Well, Jonah's emotional condition only worsened. He built a small shelter east of Nineveh and sat and waited to see what would happen to the city. God let Jonah sit and He even allowed a large, leafy plant to grow up over Jonah's shelter to give him more shade during the intense heat of the day. That made Jonah happy. Things were looking up.

But God allowed a worm to attack the plant and it withered and died. Now Jonah was more angry than ever. He was mad at the Ninevites, mad at God, mad at the worm. Nothing was working out "right." So he sang the blues, over and over again: "It would be better for me to die than to live."

How did God deal with Jonah then? He addressed the issue of Jonah's anger with a question, "Do you have a right to be angry about the vine?" Jonah replied, "I do. I am angry enough to die."

Then God asked another question that went something like this: "If you had compassion on a plant, should I not have compassion on 120,000 children?"

And we're left hanging. We don't know how Jonah responded.

What strikes me about this story is that God was not quick to try and talk Jonah out of his feelings—even when his feelings were unjustified. Throughout the book, God stayed after Jonah to teach him the right way to live, but He was not in a hurry to set Jonah straight. From whale to worm, God allowed time to be part of the process of trying to bring Jonah around. That's one way God deals with His children who are emotionally confused.

Children can't help the way they feel. But it is important for them to know what they feel and why they feel it. When they understand and accept what their feelings are, they are less likely to feel all mixed up inside. They are also less likely to feel badly toward you for not understanding them.

## TYPICAL EMOTIONAL REACTIONS OF EACH BEHAVIORAL STYLE

Different events will trigger different emotions in each DISC style. Just as weaknesses and strengths are related, so also are our fears and goals.

Whatever a person's goals are in life, her greatest fear is not reaching that goal. When goals are blocked, each style has its own emotional response and corresponding behaviors.

The goal of the "D" style is to get results. She likes to be in control and wants choices and challenges. If those goals are blocked, a "D" will become angry, impatient, demanding, and blunt. Fueled by anger, the "D" will persist in fighting for what she wants and will be insensitive to the needs of others.

The goal of the high "I" is to be liked and to have fun. She wants attention and approval. Her greatest fear, then, is loss of approval: not being liked or being left out of whatever the "in" social thing may be. When an "I" feels rejection, her emotional barometer will go from one extreme to the other—from outbursts of anger which come in the form of personal verbal attacks ("You hate my friends") to pouting and depression. It's easy for an "I" to overdraw her emotional bank account.

The goal of the "S" is to keep things peaceful and unchanged. Her fear is losing stability and security, so sudden, unplanned changes can be extremely distressing. The "S" can become locked in sadness and, as a result, give in and shut down. And she will tend to hold onto hurt feelings.

The "C" seeks to be correct. Whatever she puts her signature on, she wants it right. Her greatest fear is making mistakes or doing less than her best work. Her emotions are complex and deep. Most of the time the "C" is controlled, reserved, and seemingly emotionless. However, deep inside, the "C" may be anxious, worried, and depressed.

## NOTES

1. Adapted from Robert Bolton, *People Skills* (New York: Simon and Schuster, A Touchstone Book, 1979), 270-271.

2. Adapted from Faber and Mazlish, *How to Talk So Kids Will Listen*, 5-8. The authors highlight eight ineffective ways that people try to deal with negative feelings.

3. Haim G. Ginott, *Between Parent and Child: New Solutions to Old Problems* (New York: MacMillan, 1965), 35-36.

CHAPTER THIRTEEN

# Keep Those Loving Cups Full

Several years ago, while driving home from the office, I heard an old Dan Fogelberg song on the radio entitled, "The Loving Cup." The refrain went something like this: "Everyone is desperately seeking to fill their loving cup."

Something about that line stuck with me that night. I went home and told my family that God made all of us with a loving cup in our heart. When our loving cup is full, we feel happy and loved and we act happy. When our loving cup is low, we feel sad and act sad.

I went on to explain that when family members love each other, they keep each other's loving cups full. That night we began a ritual in the Boyd household, a tradition of asking, "Where's your loving cup today?"

So when I ask, "Callie, is your loving cup full today?" she will sometimes say "Yes," but usually at bedtime she'll say "No." I'll ask, "How full is it?" And she will point down around her ankles.

Then I'll say, "Well, let's fix that." I'll start kissing and hugging her, and she will take her hand and slowly move it up toward the top of her head. At the same time, she makes a sound like a siren that increases in pitch: "Oooooeeeeeeeee." Finally, it explodes out of the top of her head like Old Faithful: "Pssshhheeewww!"

The kids have really caught on to this ritual. They love the loving cup! One day the family was walking through the furniture section of a local department store. Suddenly Kristi stopped and said, "Daddy, my loving cup is low." We all looked at each other and then everyone looked right at me. So I got down on my knees right there in one of those aisles of couches and chairs and gave Kristi a big hug and started kissing her on the cheek until... "Pssshhheeewww!"

I asked her if anything was wrong and she said, "No. I just needed a fill-up!"

My kids even ask me where my loving cup is. Recently I arrived home from work, and Callie met me at the door. She gave me a big hug and kiss and asked, "How was your day, Dad?" I said, "Fine."

She knew that was a pretty weak answer, so she probed deeper: "But how did you *feel* today?" I said, "I felt fine."

She still wasn't satisfied. "Were you happy? Angry? Sad? Mad? Afraid? Worried? Crazy?" As she ran through this list, I made a face that corresponded to each emotion. It turned into a little guessing game, and before long we were both happy and laughing.

Then she asked me where my loving cup was. I pointed to my ankles, so she began hugging and kissing me on the cheek over and over. I slowly ran my finger up my leg, then my chest, neck, slowed down around my chin to fill up my head and then, "Pssshhheeewww!" as my loving cup ran over.

### SIMPLE, YET PROFOUND...

I've shared this idea with my congregation and at seminars. Somehow the idea catches on with people. Parents are hungry for ideas they can implement immediately in their families.

This simple, yet profound idea is a final step to affirming your child. When your child looks at the mirror in your eyes, he needs to see more than a positive reflection of his strengths and his emotions. He needs to see that you love him. I know of few ways to show your love better than physical affection.

After I began speaking about the loving cup, someone approached me and said I wasn't the first to discover this concept. In his book, *How to Really Love Your Child*, Dr. Ross Campbell talks of the same principle.

> Almost every study I know indicates that any child is continually asking his parents, "Do you love me?" A child asks this emotional question mostly in his behavior, seldom verbally. The answer to this question is absolutely the most important thing in any child's life.
>
> "Do you love me?" If we love a child unconditionally, he feels the answer to the question is yes. If we love him conditionally, he is unsure, and, again, prone to anxiety. The answer we give a child to this all-important question, "Do you love me?" pretty well determines his basic attitude toward life. It's crucial.
>
> Since a child usually asks us this question with his behavior, we usually give him our answer by what we do. By his behavior, a child tells us what he *needs*, whether it's more love, more disci-

> pline, more acceptance, or more understanding....
>
> By our behavior, we meet these needs, but we can do this only if our relationship is founded on unconditional love.... Note the phrase, "by our behavior." The feeling of love for a child in our heart may be strong. But it is not enough. By our behavior a child sees our love for him. Our love for a child is conveyed by our behavior toward that child, by what we *say* and what we *do.* But what we do carries more weight.

Then Dr. Campbell talks about each child having an *emotional tank* (sound familiar?):

> At this point, let me make one of the most important statements in this book. Only if the emotional tank is full, can a child be expected to be at his best or to do his best.

Then he asks:

> And whose responsibility is it to keep that emotional tank full? You guessed it, the parent's. A child's behavior indicates the level of the tank.... Only if the tank is kept full, can a child really be happy, reach his potential, and respond appropriately to discipline.[1]

Think about that. When your child whines, is he really asking, "Do you love me?"

When he withdraws from you, is he asking, "Do you love me?"

When he repeats a behavior that drives you up the wall, is he asking, "Do you love me?"

That's a powerful truth, isn't it? What a word picture of our responsibility as parents...to *keep their loving cups full.*

## EVERYBODY NEEDS IT

Kids need their loving cups replenished every day. Sometimes they may not act like it, but they do.

A high "I" or "S" child may ask for affection more than a "D" or "C" child, but those task-oriented little people may need it even more.

By the way, this principle applies to boys as well as girls. In our culture, when boys reach the age of five or six, their parents often decrease the times when they show their sons physical affection. But boys continue to need affectionate embraces, especially from their fathers and other men, such as grandfathers and uncles.

In a similar way, many fathers begin to pull away from their daughters after puberty. Perhaps these dads feel awkward showing affection to daughters who are suddenly blossoming into young women. But girls need physical affection from their dad during their teenage years just as much as at any other time—and perhaps more. If they don't receive it from their dad, they may look for it somewhere else. I would much rather keep my daughters' cups full than have some teenage "gorillas" do it instead.

After hearing about the loving cup at one of my seminars, one mother, Barbara, went home and put the principle into practice. Barbara told her two daughters about the loving cup and then asked Jamie (six years old and a high "D") how full her cup was. Jamie answered, "It's a little empty." So Barbara hugged and kissed her for a few seconds until Jamie said, "Okay you can stop. It's filled up to Jesus."

Then Barbara asked five-year-old Sarah (high "I") the same question. Sarah made a sad face and said, "My loving cup is empty." Barbara picked her up and began to hug and kiss her. She expected Sarah to say, "Stop," after a few seconds, but she never did.

After about two minutes, Barbara pulled back and asked, "Sarah, is your loving cup full yet?" And Sarah replied, "Oh, no, Mommy. My loving cup is deep and wide!"

Somehow I think Sarah speaks for just about every child. Whether they admit it or not!

## NOTE

1. Ross Campbell, *How to Really Love Your Child* (Wheaton, Ill.: Victor Books, 1992), 34-35.

CHAPTER FOURTEEN

# DEALING WITH CONFLICT

When you rest your head on your pillow at night and think back over a particularly difficult day with your children, how do you feel? Frustrated, fearful, unsure, unsettled, concerned, manipulated, guilty, anxious, angry, discouraged, doubtful? More than likely you wrestle with a whole complex of emotions that leaves you with nagging, unanswered questions about the way you have handled the various pressures and conflicts of the day.

You wonder if you said the right thing. Maybe you were too strict or too lenient. Could you have been more understanding, or could you have kept a conflict from occurring?

When you think about it, most of us receive little or no training in parenting. It's more difficult to obtain a driver's license than it is to become a parent. Yet how you fulfill your duty as a parent will impact your world as much as anything you do in life. Scary, isn't it?

In particular, many of us received very poor training in how to handle conflict. Our inability to work through this very natural part of family life results in broken marriages and a growing alienation between parents and children.

I cannot give you a complete guide to resolving conflict in this chapter—entire books have been written on the subject—but I can show you how the DISC model of behavioral styles will help you better understand your conflicts. In many cases, understanding the dynamics of a conflict is key to working it out—or avoiding it altogether.

### STEP ONE: UNDERSTAND THE CAUSES OF CONFLICT

The fact that each person is different makes conflict inevitable. We bring different backgrounds, viewpoints, emotions, expectations, habits, cultures, and age-related preferences into our relationships. Whenever different people come together, they will experience conflict sooner or later.

When you understand the DISC system, it's easy to spot how different behavioral styles spark conflict. At times, each core behavioral style tends to express certain attitudes and actions that can rub other people the wrong way. For example:

Directive parents and Determined children can induce conflict when they become:

- Overly concerned with their own self-interests;
- Intolerant or insensitive to the needs of others;
- Harsh, blunt, tactless communicators with others;
- Overly competitive or aggressive;
- Easily bored with necessary routines and schedules;
- Independent and detached from others;
- Too fast-paced for others to keep up with them.

Interactive parents and Influencing children can cause conflict when they:

- Clown around or lack proper seriousness;
- Talk too much or interrupt when others are talking;
- Lack attention to details and/or the necessary follow-through on tasks;
- Become too idealistic or overly optimistic;
- Are forgetful and disorganized;
- Become too excitable or emotional;
- Become verbally manipulative or allow themselves to be manipulated by peer pressure.

Supportive parents and Soft-hearted children may spark conflict when they are:

- Resistant to change and new ideas;
- Indecisive;
- Lacking initiative and a sense of urgency;
- Unable to see alternatives;
- Not assertive;
- Easily influenced; too trusting of others;
- Moving too slowly to keep pace with others.

Corrective parents and Conscientious children can cause problems when they are:

- Overly critical or judgmental of others;
- Worrying too much;

- Nosy, suspicious; asking so many detailed questions that other people feel as if they are being interrogated;
- Perfectionistic or intolerant of other's mistakes;
- Hiding or stuffing their emotions;
- Not socializing much with others;
- Stuck in the "paralysis of analysis" and moving too slowly.

Knowing that these are the natural conflict points for each behavioral style can help you experiment with strategies that minimize what might otherwise become major battlefields.

Three other principles will help you understand how differences and even similarities in behavioral styles often lead naturally to conflict:

*Conflicts arise when your differences clash.* Often, one person's strengths highlight another's weaknesses. A high "I" often will feel frustrated with a high "D" who "always wants to boss me around." A high "C" mother will grow angry at a high "S" daughter who doesn't give the same attention to important details ("important" as defined by the mother).

Sometimes one parent can have extreme difficulty relating to a child because their styles are so different that she cannot comprehend the differences.

*Conflicts can also arise when your similarities compete.* If both you and your child are high "D's," you will struggle with control issues; which one will call the shots? A high "I" mother and daughter may tend to compete for the spotlight; who gets the most attention? Two high "S's" may get along well, but will struggle if neither one takes the initiative. And two "C's" may quarrel over whose way is the "right" way.

Recently I talked with a father who has three high "D's" in his family—his wife, one of his children, and himself. As you can imagine, disagreements that would be minor rumblings in one family can become major earthquakes in this house. It's natural for three high "D" individuals to butt heads. I helped them identify these behavioral styles, but that didn't pacify the child, who moaned, "All three of us want our own way—and it's always going to be that way!"

*Realize that most people usually are not trying to do something to you, but for themselves.* Let's say you are an "S/C" parent, and you are busy trying to stay on schedule. You're in a hurry, because you have to...

- Drive to the store to purchase some groceries so you can...
- Cook your dinner by 6:00 P.M. so you can...
- Get the kids in bed at an early hour so you can...
- Watch the movie you just rented from the video store so you can...

- Make it to bed at a decent hour so you can…
- Be alert for that important presentation you have to make tomorrow.

In other words, you have the entire evening planned out. Then, in walks your "I" son who wants to tell you all about his day at school and enlist your help on his homework. After he chats for about ten minutes, you finally snap: "Can't you see that I'm trying to get some work done? Why don't you go do your homework on your own instead of always bugging me about it?"

In reality, your son has no desire to antagonize you or disrupt your schedule. He just needs to talk with someone. He's not doing something to you, but for himself, so don't take his behavior personally.

Sandra Merwin, in her book, *Figuring Kids Out,* wrote:

> When children get angry, cry, push against the rules, pout, slam doors, laugh or use any of their natural behaviors to get their needs met, parents and teachers often take it personally. Children seem to have an affinity for getting "under the skin" of the adults in their lives....
>
> Children do not get up in the morning planning how to get parents and teachers angry. Yet the child may naturally behave in such a way as to touch the most sensitive issues of the adults.[1]

Whether your conflict comes from clashing differences or competing similarities, there are some ways you can minimize the problem. I like the recommendations Bruce Narramore made in his book, *Your Child's Hidden Needs:*

First, enlist the help of your spouse. Chances are, your husband or wife is different from you and can help you gain insight and perspective into what your child is thinking or feeling.

Second, think through why your child is triggering your negative reactions. Does she remind you of yourself when you were a child? Is she like a brother or sister you fought with for years? Is she like your spouse? Or is she exactly the type of child you swore you would never raise? Whatever the reason, once you understand why that child pushes your hot button, you can become more sensitive and patient in dealing with her. You can respond, rather than react.[2]

### STEP TWO: UNDERSTAND HOW DIFFERENT PEOPLE RESPOND TO TENSION AND CONFLICT

Take a look at the chart below. Notice that under tension, a high "D" or "I" tends to vent her anger. A "D" demands that others do as she wants; she becomes overly assertive, autocratic, controlling. An "I" attacks emotionally and verbally, trying to discredit others and their ideas.

If the pressure or conflict persists, however, they may begin to suppress their emotions. When the "D" senses she cannot win, she may go to the other extreme and work alone or move to a new arena to avoid people and situations she cannot control. The "I" complies with the wishes of others in order to avoid losing social approval or just to reduce the conflict.

The initial response of the "S" and "C" styles is to suppress emotions. The "S" complies by tolerating others or giving in, while the "C" avoids the problem by withdrawing, ignoring, or planning a new strategy. And under prolonged tension, these styles may also flip-flop. The "S" will tend to vent her emotions by attacking others, while the "C" begins to demand and tries to impose her standards of "right" and "wrong" on others.

### FOUR RESPONSES TO STRESS AND CONFLICT

| | Initial Response | If Tension Persists |
|---|---|---|
| D | DEMAND | WITHDRAW |
| I | ATTACK | COMPLY |
| S | COMPLY | ATTACK |
| C | WITHDRAW | DEMAND |

This chart helps us in two keys ways. First, it helps us anticipate the natural reactions from other people so we can *respond* positively and thoughtfully, rather than *react* negatively.

Knowing how people respond to conflict will help you make wise decisions as you work through difficult situations. Let's say that a "D" father has an "I" daughter. Their conflicts probably sound something like this:

*Father:* "You need to clean your room before you go outside and play with your friends."

*Daughter:* "Dad, they're waiting for me! Can't I do it later?"

*Father:* "I'm tired of you putting these things off. You will do it now."

*Daughter:* "You didn't make Jeff clean his room before he left."

*Father:* "That was different. He had a baseball game to go to this morning. You could have done this yesterday, but you chose to watch television instead."

*Daughter:* "You are so unfair! You don't even care about me!"

*Father:* "If you don't get in there right now and clean your room, you will be staying inside the whole day!"

This type of exchange is typical of a "D" and an "I." He's becoming more demanding, and she's attacking his character in an effort to deflect the focus away from her mistake in not cleaning her room the day before. If I were the father, I would keep those behavioral styles in mind as I began the confrontation: My goal would be to keep the discussion as short as possible, to help avoid the possibility of both of us becoming more and more angry. I would not allow myself to get caught up in a verbal battle.

The chart also gives us a clue as to how much stress a person has been experiencing. If I come home from work and I find Karen in a "demand" mode, that tells me she has had a particularly difficult day. Her normal stress mode is "avoid," but under prolonged stress it can become "demand." Rather than take her reaction personally and then react to her in a way that may prolong everyone's stress and tension, I can respond by saying, "You have had a rough day, haven't you? Why don't you take some time for yourself. I'll finish up supper." I can look for ways to give her a break so that she can re-energize. (We will discuss how this is done later.)

## STEP THREE: DON'T EXPECT OTHER FAMILY MEMBERS TO THINK OR ACT LIKE YOU

At first glance, you might think this an obvious point, hardly worth mentioning. But you'd be surprised at how often this seemingly simple expectation causes problems.

Chris is the type of person who enjoys responsibility, and he likes figuring out how tasks can be completed. He feels patronized when someone shows him, step by step, how something can be done. He prefers having the freedom to figure it out for himself.

As his daughter, Jessica, grew older, Chris began giving her additional chores to perform around the house. But he couldn't understand why she never seemed to complete the tasks he assigned her. When he told her to clean her room, she did it half-heartedly, and nothing ever seemed to be put in the right place.

It seemed that Jessie had to be told exactly how to do everything—and that frustrated Chris. After all, he didn't need his parents to show him how to clean his room when he was a kid. He even planned how to use all his drawers to hold all his clothes and other belongings.

Finally, Chris realized the simple fact that Jessie didn't think and act like him. She needed to be shown what to do, slowly and specifically, step by step. Only then could she do it on her own. Whereas Chris liked figuring things out and coming up with creative solutions to problems, Jessie felt more secure when she could follow an established routine. Chris realized he needed to display more patience than normal and spend enough time with Jessie to give her the guidance she needed.

I don't agree with everything Dr. Wayne W. Dyer says in his book, *What Do You Really Want for Your Children?* but I do agree with the way he sums up the true nature of family conflicts. He writes:

> Virtually all fights revolve around the absurd thought, "If only you were more like me, then I wouldn't have to be upset." This is an erroneous assumption about the people in your world. People—including your spouse, your children, your parents, or anyone else—will never be the way you want them to be. When you find yourself upset with someone else, you are really saying to yourself, "If only you were thinking the way I am thinking right now, then I wouldn't have to be so upset." Or "Why can't you do things the way I want them to be done?"[3]

Eliminating that notion becomes a possibility when you have some way of identifying differences in style and of understanding how each member of your family needs different expressions of love and limits.

### STEP FOUR: MAKE ADJUSTMENTS TO MEET YOUR CHILDREN'S NEEDS

In chapter 9, I provided you with some very specific ways to adjust your style to meet the different needs of different children. I make this point again to underscore how important adjusting your style is to communicating love to your kids.

Both Tom and Susan are fast-paced individuals who keep very busy schedules. Their first two children, Ross and Lana, are also fast-paced. All four seem unable to relax as they move from one activity to another. Then there is Missy, the youngest daughter. She is an "S," an easygoing child who warms up slowly to new people and situations. She likes routines and familiarity. She needs a stable home environment to feel safe and secure. In fact, she can stubbornly dig her heals in to slow things down in an attempt to keep things the same.

For the longest time, Missy knew intellectually that her parents loved her, but she couldn't feel it. She felt lonely, discouraged, and unappreciated because she didn't seem to fit with the rest of the family. Looking into their "mirrors," she saw herself as weak, lazy, and unexciting.

Fortunately, all this changed when the family came to understand the DISC behavioral styles. They've learned to accept Missy's differences rather than criticize them. Realizing that God "wired" her differently and that being different is not wrong—just different—has empowered the parents to make some adjustments in how they deal with her. When they are about to make some type of change, they take more time to give Missy a picture of what the future holds. Whether they are going shopping, having company over, or changing the night of their family meetings, they make it a point to tell Missy what is going to happen ahead of time so that she has time to make the transition.

Susan puts it this way: "Over the years I've learned that for every five minutes spent in preparing Missy for how things will change, it saves me fifteen minutes of hassle. I finally realized that she isn't wasting time or whining because she wants to make my life miserable. She simply needs time to warm up and work into the change."

Another mother recently told me: "We couldn't understand why Amanda always wanted friends over or wanted to spend the night. She would be gone every night if we would let her. I wondered if we had done something wrong—if we had damaged her self-esteem in some way—since she seemed to need other people so much.

"We even tried to force her to play alone in her room, telling her she needed to slow down and enjoy being by herself sometimes. But she would become upset and angry. Now we accept her the way she is and we encourage her more. She is much happier, and it has made a big difference in her behavior. We don't have nearly as many discipline problems as before."

A family in my church has two "D/I" boys who are constantly active. One difficult time each day was dinner, because the parents could never get the boys to sit still. The two would get up and down, lean back in their chairs, or fall over. Finally, the parents bought two swivel chairs so the boys could move as much as they wanted, and dinners became much more peaceful.

I experienced this with my son, Chad, as well. Being a high "D," I look at bedtime and homework as tasks to be accomplished. Chad is a "D" as well, but he also has some "I" in him. When he was finishing up homework just before bedtime, for example, I would come in to quiz him on some science questions to prepare for the next day's test. After each question, Chad would want to stop and talk and tell me a story. My goal was to get the work done so we could both go to bed. His goal was to talk and have a good time with his dad. I was afraid that he was taking advantage of me, manipulating me to stay up longer. But was that really true? Sometimes it could be. But chances are, he didn't intentionally attempt to get to stay up longer. He wasn't trying to do something to me. He was acting naturally for his style.

No matter how deeply you love your children, loving them is not enough. Your love must soak in. They must feel loved, and that means adjusting your style to better meet their needs. If you don't adjust your style, you may send a message to that "different" child that she is a bother to you, that something is wrong with her since she is not like you. Counselors' offices are filled with people whose parents loved them, but who, for whatever reason, were not able to experience deeply their parents' love. No matter how different or difficult your child seems to be, you must make adjustments. You must learn to compliment and enjoy each child for who they are.

### STEP FIVE: GIVE EACH FAMILY MEMBER THE OPPORTUNITY TO RECHARGE

You may not realize you have a power cord hanging out of your lower back. Not a tail, a power cord. Go ahead. Look in a mirror. It's there.

For you to function effectively each day, you must plug your power cord into certain activities that energize you. Your spouse and your kids also have this same power cord.

It costs you energy to adjust your style to meet other people's needs. As parents we are called on to change the way we relate to our children to meet their needs. But any time you push yourself out of your natural comfort zone and into behaviors which are not a part of your natural style, you'll feel some stress. And stress tends to deplete your mental, emotional, and physical energy.

When your energy levels are low, you are less patient, less flexible, and more obstinate. In other words, the less energy you have, the more likely you will end up in conflict with someone else. This means that the more you are able to give yourself and your child the opportunity to recharge your batteries, the less conflict you'll experience.

In general, a drain on energy reserves occurs when:

• The more task-oriented parenting styles (Directive, Corrective) are called upon to express more people-related interaction;

• The people-oriented styles (Interactive, Supportive) adjust to become more task-focused;

• The slower-paced people (Supportive, Corrective) have to speed up; or the fast-paced people (Directive, Interactive) are made to slow down.

Adequate physical rest is one important way for you to recharge your batteries. But if you think about it, you'll also recognize certain activities which consistently help you relieve stress and renew your energy. Chances are that these activities are directly related to your behavioral style.

There are definite warning signs to watch for—symptoms that will alert you to the fact that you or your child is suffering from stress. Generally, a high "D" or "I" will become loud, demanding, and hyperactive. An "S" turns quiet and withdraws emotionally, and a "C" will grow picky and whiny—she will focus on something that bothers her and won't let go of it. It's like she gets into a "loop" that she can't get out of.

Identifying these activities for you and your children will allow you to avoid many conflicts in your home. By making recharging a priority, your family members will be calmer, happier, and less likely to lash out at someone for minor infractions.

A high "D" needs to burn off stress like a locomotive burns coal. This means doing something physical—whether it be playing tennis, mowing the lawn, building a retaining wall in the back yard, or clearing about one hundred acres or so of forested land. It's almost a compulsion. She'll come home from a difficult day of people interaction at the office and exclaim, "If I don't get out and exercise, I'll go nuts!"

A high "I" recharges by being with people and by talking. You can see it in her eyes. Put her in a room full of people or give her one attentive ear, and she comes alive.

High "I" mothers who stay at home with young children will experience great frustration if they don't have enough interaction with adults. Robin recently shared with her parenting group, "Interacting with my children just doesn't fulfill my people needs. I love being at home with my children. They're great! But now that I know I'm a high "I" and high "I's" need to talk and be with people, I'm planning more outings with other moms. During my kids' nap time, I'm using the telephone to stay more connected with my friends. My energy level is much higher. Even my husband has noticed the difference, and he's helping me arrange more time away with my friends."

A high "S" usually finds that "nothing time"—relaxing—will energize her. This may mean fishing, a bubble bath, watching television, or walking and/or talking with a close friend. For many "S's," nothing time means sleeping late or going to bed early. Many stay-at-home moms find it helpful to take a quick nap, even if it means peanut butter and jelly for supper.

A high "C" needs private time to recharge. She enjoys a quiet evening with a book in front of a fireplace, listening to classical music, working on a project, or a day in a bookstore. She needs time alone to think, process, and percolate.

One of the most interesting men I've known, I met in Australia on a mission trip. Dr. John Hercus was a high "C" who loved to think deeply about the why's of spiritual life, and he wrote several books. What surprised me was learning that many of his best creative ideas came while working in his yard. His yard work was his private think time. It became the seed bed of ideas for most of his books and his philosophy of life.

### ENERGY AND YOUR KIDS

Understanding energy needs is important for kids, as well. When their energy levels are low, kids have a harder time coping with circumstances that don't fit their natural style. They will be more self-centered and harder to get along with. However, when energy levels are high, kids have more power to express their strengths and cope with uncomfortable situations.

Consider, for example, the condition your children find themselves in when they arrive home from school. They've been interacting with people all day, but they've also been sitting at their desks, completing tasks, and staying quiet (hopefully!). If you don't realize what they need to recharge when they return home, you'll set yourself up for some heated conflicts later on.

After a day like this, "S" and "C" children will be worn out from having to interact in groups of people. They may need to be alone to recharge. They'll want to play alone in their rooms, read books, or watch television. They may not need a lot of time before they're ready to head outside to play, but they probably will need some.

Forget trying to get these children to tell you how their day at school went the moment they walk in the door. More than likely, it will be bedtime before they are ready to talk. You may have to patiently ask many questions to draw them out.

High "D" kids will arrive home ready for action. They've been sitting all day, and they have energy to burn. The last thing you want to do with a "D" child is make her complete her homework before she goes outside to play.

"I" children draw energy from others. If they have not had enough people interaction on a particular day at school, they will need the opportunity to talk and interact with you or with friends.

One high "C" mom related this story about after-school conflicts: "After spending the day interacting with people at work, I'm ready for some time alone. I need peace and I need space. But just about the time I begin to relax, in comes my high "I" son and daughter. (Did you catch that? This high "C" mom has two high "I" children. We're talking a major drain on energy reserves just to deal with these kids!)

"When they walk through the door, they are ready to recount their entire day, starting from the time I dropped them off at school. I worried that something was wrong with me. I'd cut the kids off and even yell at them unjustly. I didn't understand why I was reacting the way I was.

"Now I realize they've been made to sit, listen, and be quiet most of the day, so I know they need to talk and move to recharge their batteries. But I also know that I need time alone. What we do is sit down together, have a snack, and talk for twenty minutes. I can listen that long. Then they go outside to play with their friends until supper. That way, most of the time I have some alone time until dinner is served."

When you discern what it is your children need to recharge, you'll begin to make similar adjustments in how you treat them.

"I couldn't figure out why Sarah would disappear into her room whenever we had someone spend the day with us," one mother told me. "Now I know she is a high "C," and she needs time alone to recharge. Giving her time to herself and not trying to force her to talk when I'm ready to talk has helped us all get along better."

On another occasion, I worked with a large family to help them understand their behavioral styles and how each person interacted with the others.

Their teenage daughter, Ashley, is an "I/C," and she commented, "I used to worry that something was wrong with me. There are times when I just don't want to be with this family. (Remember, she has polar opposite internal needs. The "I" wants to be on the go and to be with people; the "C" part of her needs to move more slowly and needs time alone to process.) Now I realize that wanting to be by myself sometimes is okay. It's the high "C" part of me that needs time alone."

The father asked Ashley's younger brother, Benjamin, what they could do to help Ashley feel encouraged. Benjamin replied, "I guess we need to listen to her." Being a high "D," however, he added a bit of frustration from years of listening to his high "I" sister's long stories: "But Dad, I don't want to go to China to get to New York!" (Is that a "D" or what? Does he understand an "I"?)

## Make Recharging a Priority

Once you see how recharging your emotional batteries will reduce tension in your home, you shouldn't have any problem realizing how important it is. The difficulty is making time for it in your schedule. You need to place a high priority on planning regular, consistent times to recharge.

Donald Tubesing, author of *Kicking Your Stress Habit*, puts it this way: "It would be nice if we could eat a side of beef, drink a barrel of water, and have our nutritional needs met for a month, but that doesn't happen. We have to meet our needs on a daily basis."[4] This is especially true of our energy needs. If you are a "D," you must plan some physical time. If you are a high "I," you must deliberately arrange your schedule so that you can have your people needs met. If you are an "S," you need "nothing time" to recharge. If you are a "C," you must plan time alone.

In a very real sense, you must nurture yourself so you can nurture your child.

If you can't remember the last time you took time for yourself or left your kids with a sitter so you could go out with friends, it's time to recharge. Don't allow your batteries to run so low that you have nothing left to give to those you care about most.

And when your child begins misbehaving, make a mental check of her energy level. Does she need a recharge? How can you help her recharge?

Of all the practical advice I could give you about handling conflict, this may be the easiest for you to implement. It also may bring the quickest results.

## NOTES

1. Sandra Merwin, *Figuring Kids Out* (Minnetonka, Minn.: TigerLily Press, 1992), 117-118.

2. Bruce Narramore, *Your Child's Hidden Needs* (Old Tappan, N.J.: Fleming H. Revell, 1990), 29-30.

3. Wayne Dyer, *What Do You Really Want for Your Children?* (New York: Avon Books, 1985), 197.

4. Donald Tubesing, *Kicking Your Stress Habit* (New York: Penguin, 1982).

CHAPTER FIFTEEN

# PARENTS ARE ALSO PARTNERS

Perhaps the greatest single thing I remember about my father while I was growing up was that he loved my mother. Every night when he arrived home from work, he would immediately walk into the kitchen, put his arms around my mom, give her a big kiss, and tell her how much he loved her. I can still see that scene as if it were yesterday.

When I think of my childhood, I realize that my parents gave me a great gift: They showed me that two people could live together in love and unity but at the same time be very different.

This is a book about parenting, but it's clear to me that, if you want to become a better parent, strengthening your marriage is a good place to start.

A recent study by the Timberlawn Psychiatric Research Foundation of Dallas, Texas, found that, for children to develop normally, they need strong parents united in their love for each other. "No matter what you say or do directly to your children, a well-functioning marriage bathes them in an amber glow of something very positive, so that they grow up very, very strong and healthy," says John T. Gossett, the Timberlawn director. "A marriage in constant conflict bathes the child in some kind of bright-red heat of misery that's very damaging."[1]

Before your kids feel you value their uniqueness, you must demonstrate that you understand and appreciate your spouse's strengths and accept the ways in which he is different from you.

Just as understanding the DISC behavioral styles can help you become a better parent, it also can help strengthen your marriage. It may be one of the greatest discoveries of your married life.

### WHO IS THIS WOMAN I MARRIED?

Karen and I dated off and on for four years, but it was not until we married that I discovered the terrible truth: Karen was strange. She just wasn't normal—at least, not like I was.

It started on our wedding night. The temperature on our July wedding day reached almost 100 degrees. When we arrived at the hotel that night in Daytona Beach, Florida, the first thing I did was turn the air conditioner on high. As I showered, Karen was shivering, so she turned the air off! When I came out of the bathroom, I began sweating and turned the air conditioning back on high.

We discovered that night that our inner thermostats just don't match. This made for an interesting beginning to our honeymoon! I didn't know it then, but this proved to be a foreshadowing of our life together.

Soon after that, we started furnishing our first home. You know a young couple is in trouble when they start out to buy furniture and she says, "Ethan Allen?" and he replies, "Who's that, your uncle?" With that, I discovered that Karen's and my tastes were completely different.

Our styles of handling finances also differ. I make money to spend money. She makes money to save it. I don't want to knock myself out working and not be able to enjoy life. She doesn't want to wake up one morning when we are sixty-five and find nothing in our retirement fund.

Before we were married, if a couple of checks bounced at the bank, I would simply switch banks and start all over. Karen actually is excited when she receives the monthly bank statement so she can balance the check book to the penny.

My father-in-law, now a retired army colonel, kept his family on their toes. Even today, when we visit, he's always busy with some project—installing a new kitchen, changing the light fixtures in the bathroom, re-landscaping the front yard.

Karen follows in his footsteps. She's not happy unless she's refinishing furniture, putting in a new flower bed, or sewing curtains for the kids' rooms.

My dad, meanwhile, worked from sunup to sundown building houses. When he came home, the last thing he wanted to do was work around the house. So guess whom I take after? For me, home means rest and relaxation.

You can imagine the kinds of conflicts Karen and I began having soon after we were married. Karen just couldn't understand why I didn't want to work on projects around the house. After all, that's what she enjoyed, and that's what her father (her role model for a man) enjoyed as well.

The differences don't end there. Karen and I operate from different inner motors. I always like to arrive early to any appointment or event. Karen is usually late. Before she leaves the house, she wants to make sure everything left behind is just right, and that takes time.

On vacation, Karen loves to drive slowly, stopping at outlet malls along the way and at hotels for a leisurely overnight stay. For me, the fun begins when you get where you're going; the drive is not the vacation but a necessary evil. I've been known to drive twenty-two hours straight home, carrying an empty mayonnaise jar so we don't have to make so many bathroom stops.

## AND THEN GOD STEPPED IN

I don't know how Karen and I were so blind to all this before our wedding. I guess we were just a typical couple with stars in our eyes. Somewhere between our honeymoon and the birth of our first child, we woke up to a disturbing revelation: We were really *very* different. And these differences began to cause quite a bit of friction.

For ten years I truly believed that if Karen were more like me she would be happier and we could have a great marriage. Of course, she thought the same about me. So we chipped away at each other, trying to remake the other into our own image.

Fortunately, God intervened. Through attending a leadership seminar in a nearby church, I was exposed to the DISC model that you have been learning about. The instrument we took at that time was called the Performax Personal Profile System. I later applied this system to marriage, and the Carlson Learning Company published it as The Couples' Profile. It allows two people to see how they are alike and how they are different. (See the resource section at the back of this book for more information on these helpful profiles.)

When Karen and I charted our behavioral styles, here is how we looked. (I am the dark dots; Karen the white.) As you can see, we are quite different!

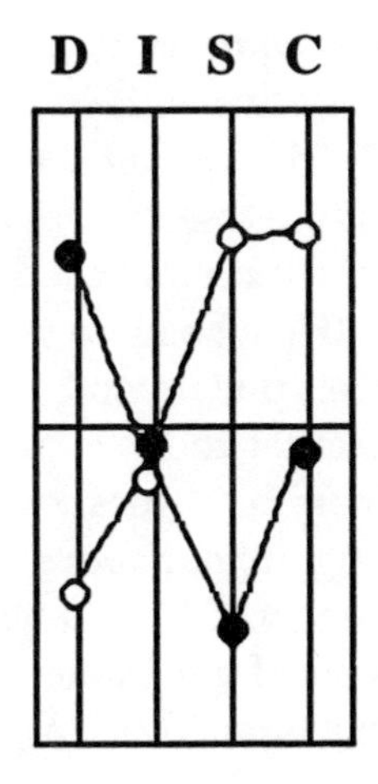


I knew we were different, but now I had objective evidence. What had previously been unidentifiable points of conflict and tension suddenly became clearly defined areas that we could discuss. Our different paces, for example, were identified as typical of our behavioral styles.

For us, this information felt like that first fresh autumn breeze after a hot and humid summer. It made a permanent difference in our relationship.

- It laid to rest once and for all the belief that there is one "normal" way of being.
- We gained a better understanding of ourselves—who we are as the unique individuals God made us.
- We learned how we are alike and how we are different, and how those similarities and differences affect our relationship. This understanding enables us to anticipate potential conflict and go deeper than surface issues when conflict occurs.
- We learned how we could adjust our style to specifically meet the other's needs.
- We began to not only accept each other, but to appreciate and value our differences as well. That empowered us to be the people God created each of us to be.

I now had a choice. I could: A) stubbornly continue to try to change Karen to be more like me in order to meet my needs, or B) make voluntary and loving changes to better meet her needs. Choice B was the only logical option if we wanted a loving, lasting marriage.

## SEVEN WAYS TO USE DISC TO ENHANCE YOUR MARRIAGE

For the past six years, we've worked toward our goal of oneness in marriage by valuing the ways in which we are different. Oneness does not mean sameness. Oneness is unity in diversity. In the process, we've discovered at least seven practical ways to use this tool to enhance our marriage:

First, **work at understanding your spouse.** Peter instructed husbands to "live with your wives in an understanding way" (1 Peter 3:7, NASB). This principle applies to wives as well. Understanding each other is the essential first step to reducing marital friction.

Paul Tournier stated it this way in his book, *To Understand Each Other*: "He who loves understands, and he who understands loves. One who feels understood feels loved. And one who feels loved, feels sure of being understood."[2]

There is no question a direct link exists between love and understanding. If your spouse does not feel understood, he will not feel loved. Alan, an "S/C," is a university professor and author. He enjoys long moments of quiet time alone for reading and meditating. His wife, Susan, a high "D/C," is just the opposite. An active, industrious type, she loves to cross things off her "to do" list. When Susan begins to feel overwhelmed at the amount of things she has set her mind to accomplish, she enlists Alan's help. "Since you're not doing anything," she declares, "come and help me hang these pictures."

Not doing anything? How do you think Alan feels? Offended...and misunderstood.

Truly understanding your spouse means that you must discover how he is uniquely different from you. Just as you became a student of your child, you also become a student of your spouse. Paula Rinehart put it this way: "We are always growing toward the understanding that the person we married does not innately think and respond as we would. He is a different person, a mystery well worth unraveling."[3]

One night, one of the elders in our church invited me to go hear a jazz guitarist in concert. About thirty minutes into the show, my friend leaned over and said, "Are those people talking behind us bothering you?"

I hadn't noticed them until that point, but after that I noticed a constant buzz as these people whispered to each other. It got so irritating that finally my friend leaned back and nicely but assertively said, "You know, if you folks want to talk, would you mind scooting down a few seats?"

The man replied, "Oh, I'm sorry. You see my wife is blind and I was just telling her about what was happening on stage."

Talk about a change in attitude! We both looked at each other and slumped down in our chairs, feeling foolish.

What made the difference? We understood what was really going on. When we did, our annoyance and judgment melted away.

This shift in attitude also occurs when you work at understanding your spouse. Make an effort to study your spouse's moods, mannerisms, likes and dislikes, strengths and weaknesses. Take note of what pleases him and upsets him...and when he needs encouragement. Get to know what makes him tick, and what ticks him off.

This is one course you never graduate from, so consider yourself a life-long learner.

Second, **accept your spouse just as he is**. There's one truth you need to engrave on your mind: *Different is not wrong…just different.*

You need to make a choice to lovingly accept your spouse's differences and not maintain an agenda to change him.

After a recent seminar, a woman thanked me for how much the session had helped her. "It helped me understand my daughter," she said. "Heather is my clone—not that I made her that way. That's just the way she is."

Then she continued: "But the best thing about the seminar was that it helped me understand and accept myself. My husband is always telling me that I'm crazy. He says nobody thinks the way I do. Now I know there is nothing wrong with the way I am. There are a lot of people like me."

I was happy for what this woman had learned about herself, but I really wished that her husband could have attended the seminar as well.

Another man, so stuck in his way of seeing things, wrote on a conference evaluation, "I was surprised to find that there were so many other people in the world like my wife that they deserved their own special category."

Both of these husbands need to accept their wives for who they are. They need to realize that different is not wrong...just different. Along with every other married partner, they need to clearly and consistently send the message, "You don't have to change for me to love you. It's okay to be who you are."

Third, **return to your "before marriage" perspective of your spouse**. You were attracted to your partner because of certain strengths and character qualities. For example, before marriage a young woman might be attracted to a man with a high "D" style because he is decisive, independent, determined, and courageous. However, after marriage she may begin to feel troubled by his negative attributes. Now he seems impatient, uncaring, stubborn, and reckless.

Chris ("I/D") was a life-of-the-party salesman who always had something to say. Mary ("S/C"), a more reserved type, felt uncomfortable in large groups, and she was attracted to Chris right away because he had such self-confidence. She thought Chris was outgoing, charming, talkative, and witty.

Six years after their marriage, Mary came for counseling, deeply depressed. She wanted a perfect marriage, but Chris didn't do things "right." He was often late for supper, which she always had ready on time, and she took his tardiness as a personal insult. She could not believe that he was not as time-conscious as she was, so she felt he was late on purpose. But she did not discuss the problem with him because she didn't want to cause friction.

After attending a few parties with Chris, she realized he told the same corny jokes over and over. She also got tired of spending thirty minutes trying to pull him away from other people at these gatherings; it seemed he never wanted to leave, and he didn't appreciate the fact that she didn't enjoy these parties as much as he did.

When Chris told his side of the story, he painted another picture.

"Mary is a sweet, tender-hearted girl, and I love that part of her. But she's been depressed half the time since we got married. She used to think I was funny—as everyone does—but now she's getting tired of me.

"If I come home ten minutes late, she's upset. She can't seem to understand that I'm a salesman, and I can't rush my customers just so I can keep to my wife's schedules. I feel like I've married my mother, and I'm always a bad little boy."

This problem is a matter of perspective. Mary wants to maintain familiar routines and schedules. Chris is a people-person, and time just seems to slide by. One is not right and the other wrong; *the perspectives are just different!*

As you learned in chapter 10, many frustrating traits of the people you love are the flip side of the qualities you most appreciate. They are strengths pushed to an extreme. What once attracted you to your spouse may now be the point of attack.

Time and familiarity have a way of causing you to begin to focus on the negatives rather than the positives. Go back and look at those wedding pictures again. Return to your "before marriage" view.

Fourth, **realize that every couple combination has potential problems**. We have all heard that opposites attract. When we look at our partner's strengths, it is a great asset to have opposites united. However, even though opposites attract, they may eventually attack. When couples are different in any one of the four DISC dimensions, they may have problems.

A high "D"/low "D" couple may have conflicts when they make decisions. The high "D" wants to decide and decide now, but the low "D" wants to put off making a decision. The high "D" tends to make independent decisions. The low "D" desires a more democratic approach to decision-making.

When a high "I" is coupled with a low "I," they may also experience some tension. Generally speaking, the high "I" is *generally speaking*. The low "I" is more reserved, keeping his thoughts and feelings to himself. Communication (or lack of it) could become an area of conflict. The low "I" may see the high "I" as being superficial; the high "I" may see the low "I" as inexpressive.

The high "S"/low "S" combination may struggle over the issue of change: The high "S" wants things to remain the same and the low "S" is more spontaneous, wanting change for change's sake and to spice things up.

The high "C"/low "C" pair may wrestle with attention to key

details. The high "C" is more cautious and conscientious and makes his decisions based on lots of facts. Friction can occur in this relationship because the low "C" tends to go with his gut reaction to things and has the attitude, "Don't sweat the small stuff."

Many marital conflicts arise because we don't appreciate that our spouse has different strengths than we do. What we don't understand, we fail to appreciate. What we don't understand often puts us off. It confuses us and may even offend or threaten us. That's why understanding your DISC style can lead to a more caring relationship.

Just as opposites attract in some marriages, "birds of a feather flock together" in others. Occasionally people of similar styles come together because they tend to approach life in the same way and find that satisfying. Nonetheless, feathers are ruffled in these marriages as well.

When both husband and wife are high "D" styles, they know where they are going and how to get there, but each one wants to be in control. This couple may experience titanic power struggles.

Two high "I's" can have a great deal of fun together, but they may compete for the "out front" position. They may try to outdo each other for first place. Who looks better? Who's in the spotlight? Two high "I's" may also become so overwhelmed by outside commitments that they forget to take time for each other. They risk developing a superficial relationship that lacks the solid foundation of intimacy.

Two "S" spouses may agree on matters like establishing familiar routines and keeping their home and family on an even keel. However, their desire for an emotionally secure, conflict-free family may cause conflict as each waits for the other to make decisions or to assume responsibilities. Initiative is the conflict issue here. Who will decide? Who is willing to take a risk?

Two high "C's" may agree on their commitment to excellence. But they may get caught in a competition over competency: Whose way is the right way? Also, with their analytical minds, they may take some arguments too seriously and begin a silent battle in which each judges the other's values and motives and blows the conflict out of proportion.

No matter what behavioral style combination you have in your marriage, one critical commitment is important: your willingness to work together to improve your marriage.

After a couples workshop, a woman showed me how she and her husband had scored on a DISC instrument, "The Couples Profile." They were opposite in every way, and she asked, "Should we just give up? We're so different." I explained the following point, which has since become a cornerstone principle in every marriage workshop I'm involved with:

*In marriage, compatibility is no longer the issue.* Commitment *is the issue.*

Any two people who love and accept each other and who are willing to work together can have a good marriage—one that improves over time. It doesn't depend on how alike or how different you are. It depends on how *willing* you are.

Fifth, **don't take your partner's behavior personally**. Does this point sound familiar? It should, because I also listed it in the previous chapter. It's worth repeating because so many marriage problems can be neutralized by understanding this simple principle.

When you realize that your partner's actions result from his natural style of relating, rather than being a tactic designed to anger or offend you, then his behavior will no longer be interpreted as a threat or an affront.

This point came home to me several years ago in a counseling session. The couple was almost alike in every category except one. Megan was a high "I," and Jack a low "I." They were encountering a good deal of stress in their marriage, which they attributed to Jack's high stress job and their tight financial condition.

When I looked at their graphs, I suspected that some other problems lurked beneath the surface. "Megan, I bet you're feeling rejected in this marriage," I said. She replied, "You're right. That's the problem in our marriage."

Then I looked at Jack and said, "I bet you're feeling smothered." He said, "That is the real problem in the marriage." Both couldn't believe I had hit the nail on the head so quickly.

As a high "I," Megan wanted to talk things out when she felt stressed. That made Jack feel smothered. His style of handling stress was to think things through—by heading out into the woods. Guess how that made Megan feel? Right. Rejected.

When I explained the principle that "most people do what they do, not because they are trying to do something *to you*, but because they're doing something *for themselves*," I could see the lights flash on in their heads. They smiled, their shoulders relaxed, and both of them let out a deep sigh. With this new insight, both became more willing to give the other what that person needed.

Sixth, **learn to adjust your style to meet your partner's needs**. Rather than expecting your spouse to change to meet your needs, you take the initiative. You change to meet *his* needs.

When Jack and Megan realized that their partner's actions were not designed as a personal attack, they were more free to make loving adjustments in their relationship. Megan began to let Jack have his time alone to process his thoughts and feelings, and Jack agreed to sit down and talk with Megan right after his think time so that they could talk out the problem and make decisions.

The idea of changing is one that runs cross-grain to many people. I'm not saying you need to change because there is something inherently wrong with your natural style. Instead, you should attempt to relate to others in ways that are the most accepting, approving, and encouraging to them.

This approach means going beyond your own needs to meet the needs of your spouse. It's one of the most practical methods I know of living out the command of Philippians 2:3-4:

> Do nothing out of selfish ambition or vain conceit, but in humility consider others better than yourselves. Each of you should look not only to your own interests, but also to the interests of others.

Changing your spouse is not the goal, but marriage will change you. You become more unselfish, other-focused, and willing to adjust to meet the other's need.

Finally, **remember that God has made you a team, and your team is stronger because of your differences**. God put you together to complete one another and to accomplish His purposes for your lives together.

When God first created man, He saw that something was not right. "It is not good for the man to be alone," God said. "I will make a helper suitable for him" (Genesis 2:18). The woman God created was designed just for Adam, as a helper.

For many married couples, this is an amazing thought. I can hear it now: "You mean I'm supposed to be glad for my partner's weaknesses?" Yes, and he should be glad for all of yours as well!

Now if you and your partner are different as husband and wife, chances are you will not deal with your children in the same way, either.

A friend recently told me about the day he came home from work and found his five-year-old son on top of their minivan, trying to hammer a nail through a six-foot-long two-by-four and into the roof. The father's natural reaction (he's a "D/C") was to grab the kid off the top of the car and take immediate disciplinary steps to ensure that this would not happen again.

As he entered the house with his son under his arm, he was met by his wife. Her response (she's an "I/S") was, "Well, did you ever specifically tell him he couldn't hammer nails on top of the car?" His response was, "No, there are certain things he ought to know." Their differing styles became apparent. He wanted the little carpenter restricted to his room for the next twelve years. She preferred leniency.

Here were two parents looking at the same situation, the same child, the same incident, but they drew opposite conclusions. The dad wanted to nail him, the mom wanted to nurture him. Together they are much more effective as parents than either would be alone. In the end, the dad decided to talk sternly with his son, explaining why this was not appropriate behavior and warning him that, if it happened again, he would be punished.

*Partners who understand, accept, and appreciate each other's similarities and differences make the most effective parenting team.*

### CHERISHING THE DIFFERENCES

Adjusting to another person, particularly one with a behavioral style opposite yours, is not easy, and it is not done quickly. But like anything of real value, the payoff to your relationship is worth the investment.

Bill and Lynn Hybels discovered this, and he shares about it in his book, *Honest to God?:*

> The same differences that used to hinder our relationship now enhance it. What we tried so hard to change, we now cherish.... Lynn and I could have avoided years of frustration if we had realized that we weren't better or worse than one another—just different. When you accept and quit passing moral judgment on those differences, you open the door for workable compromise. You end up delighting in the very differences that once caused you division.[4]

Karen and I are continually learning how our differences are not deficits; they are the very things God uses to make us a stronger team.

I need Karen's attention to detail and she needs my ability to see the big picture. I need her sense of structure and security; she needs my spontaneity. She appreciates my quicker decision-making ability; I appreciate her more cautious approach. I'm learning the value of saving for retirement; she's learning to spend money. (I'm not sure I win with that one!) Our tastes in furniture are beginning to mesh. I still want to relax; she still wants to landscape the front yard.

But what a difference our differences have made! Karen has blossomed as a woman, a wife, a mother, and is even pushing herself out of her comfort zone to speak with me at FamilyLife Marriage Conferences. And I am learning I need Karen's strengths. She brings to my life qualities that I lack. I can't tell you how many times her more cautious nature has reminded me to slow down and look at things more closely, and it has saved me big bucks as well.

Our differences have also helped us become a more effective parenting team. Her more supportive/corrective style is a good balance to my directive style. Her slower approach gives stability to the family, and my faster approach gets us to the beach in Florida faster.

I probably could have married someone with a style more similar to mine. But since I met Karen, I couldn't imagine loving anyone as much. She is God's gift to me.

Even if she still keeps turning the thermostat up!

**NOTES**

1. Annie Gottlieb, "The Secret Strength of Happy Marriages," *McCall's* (December 1990): 94.

2. Paul Tournier, *To Understand Each Other,* trans. John S. Gilmour (Atlanta: John Knox Press, Pillar Books, 1977), 28.

3. Paula Rinehart, "Two of a Kind?" *Discipleship Journal,* no. 46 (1988): 5.

4. Bill Hybels, *Honest to God?* (Grand Rapids, Mich.: Zondervan, 1990), 74.

# AFTERWORD

Occasionally, after a Child's Design workshop or class, a parent will come up and say something like this: "But I don't want to have to think about all this. I just want to look at my kid and say, 'Do this,' and my child does it, or 'Don't do that,' and have him obey."

That *would* be great, wouldn't it? Unfortunately, parenting doesn't work that way, as you well know. There's no doubt that parenting is hard work. As family therapist Virginia Satir put it: *I regard this [parenting] as the hardest, most complicated, anxiety-ridden, sweat and blood producing job in the world.*[1]

But let me go back and remind you of the big picture before we close. We have said that Proverbs 22:6 commands parents to nurture their kids according to their nature. We have also said that to do that effectively, you must know how God has designed you, as well as know your child's unique bent. You must become a student of your child by looking for the bent behind the behavior.

My favorite Christian writer and speaker is Chuck Swindoll. His combination of wit and wisdom has both instructed and encouraged me time and again for over a decade. He powerfully sums up what we have been saying in his book *The Strong Family*:

When it comes to rearing children, developing a strong home where happiness and harmony can flourish, there is a primary starting point: *knowing your child.* This is the most profound insight, the single most helpful secret I can pass on to you on the subject of child-rearing."2

What makes his statement even more significant is what he goes on to say a few pages later:

> One of my first books was *You and Your Child.* In it I presented some of these principles in greater detail than I have attempted to do here....

> I mention that because over fifteen years have passed since I first put those ideas into print. Back then our four were small. The principles I suggested were in a somewhat embryonic and theoretical stage as Cynthia and I were in the process of putting them to work. All four of our children are now in their twenties and early thirties (three of them married and rearing their own children), our youngest is continuing his education. Our four are no longer little children. We have had occasion to see if the ideas presented way back then still hold water. I am so grateful to report they work! Now that we have had ample opportunity to try these things out in the crucible of everyday living, it is a great joy (and relief) to announce that the truth of God's counsel has paid off. The principles are paying off...so far!"

(The ideas and principles to which he refers are based on the same interpretation of Proverbs 22:6 as we have set forth in this book and on the basic premise, knowing your child.) Swindoll then states the key concept again:

> If parents were to ask me, "What is the greatest gift we could give our child?" ...my counsel to you would be, give your child the time it takes to find out how he or she is put together. Help your child know who he or she is. Discuss those things with your children. Help them know themselves so that they learn to love and accept themselves as they are. Then, as they move into a society that seems so committed to pounding them into another shape, they will remain true to themselves, secure in their independent walk with their God.

He concludes with these words:

> I have begun to realize that secure, mature people are best described in fifteen words: they know who they are...they like who they are...they are who they are...they are *real.*"[3]

Who could say it better than "The Sermonater"?

That is the biblical big picture: Know your child, accept your child, and help your child know himself. That's what it means to train your child up according to his bent. That's what it takes for your child to grow up and be true to his God-given design. As I said at the beginning of this book, there is much more to parenting than what we've discussed in these pages. But you must begin here.

How do you practically carry out your charge? I believe the DISC model gives us a language to describe the differing bents we find in our kids, and it does so in a very understandable way. It also provides us with insights on how we can adjust our style to better meet our children's needs.

Parenting by design takes time, effort, and most of all, desire. But these ideas and principles are do-able. I trust the payoff will be worth it for us all.

## NOTES

1. Virginia Satir, *Peoplemaking* (Palo Alto, Calif.: Science and Behavior Books, 1972), 197.

2. Charles Swindoll, *The Strong Family* (Portland, Ore.: Multnomah Press, 1991), 61.

3. Ibid., 66-67.

# FORTY BEHAVIORAL STRENGTHS YOU CAN MIRROR TO YOUR CHILD

As I discussed in chapter 11, your child's self-image will depend largely on what you reflect to him. Your challenge is to reinforce his positive qualities, using descriptive praise to let him know the good things about how God has designed him.

In this section, you'll find forty different behavioral traits—ten for each of the "D," "I," "S," and "C" styles. For each character quality, you will find some encouraging words which you can use to affirm your child or anyone else with those qualities. *These words are presented as if you were talking with your child.* In addition, I've also briefly noted some related weaknesses—strengths taken to extremes—for you to use when correcting your child.

Look for everyday opportunities to use these qualities to encourage your child. And keep in mind that this is a *template*. There are no magic formulas. These are suggested examples for you to experiment with. Develop your own way of saying these things.

Also, look closely at *how* things are said, not just *what* is said. In some cases, the character quality points to how this trait will help the child in the future. With others, a balancing strength is mentioned. As you begin to use descriptive praise, vary your style so your encouragement doesn't sound canned.

Read through all forty qualities rather than concentrating just on your child's dominant style. Remember that each individual is a blend of different styles; if your child is a high "I," you may notice he also has qualities listed here under "D," and so on.

Further, because human behavior fluctuates, from time to time you will see your child express the behavior strengths of other styles. When this happens, be sure to make a mental and verbal note. Let your child know that it is possible to develop skills in areas that don't come naturally.

Much of the following information is adapted from two resources developed by Wes Neal: "Seventy Positive Qualities for the Profile of Appreciation" (1988), and "Turning Weaknesses into Strengths" (1989). I am deeply indebted to Wes for permitting me to include his material. If you would like to know more about *The Profile of Appreciation* and about Wes's ministry, contact: Champions of Excellence, P.O. Box 627, Branson, MO 65616. Or call 417-334-7037.

# PRAISEWORTHY QUALITIES OF THE HIGH "D" IN YOUR LIFE

### ASSERTIVE

You are able to take action in situations when other people are hesitant or are looking for a way out. As an assertive person, you can meet a challenge head on without having to be told again and again to do something. In fact, you're the kind of person who can find pleasure in tackling difficult assignments—you see them as challenges that will stretch your abilities.

Assertiveness, balanced with being sensitive to other people's feelings, is a great strength, especially as you use it to meet the needs of other people.

*Related weaknesses: insensitivity, lacks empathy.*

### DETERMINED

Determination is a great strength that achievers share. It means you can make up your mind to do something, and you won't stop until you get it done! Sure, there will be plenty of obstacles, but your determination will somehow find a way over, around, or through them.

One building block of determination is maintaining an open mind to better ideas and better ways to do what you're doing. So, unlike the stubborn person who says, "I'm sticking to my original plan no matter what!" you are open to plans and ideas that help you get the job done.

Your determination can be an inspiration to others. It shows that God can sharpen a person's mind to see ways around the roadblocks!

*Related weaknesses: overbearing, domineering, headstrong.*

### DILIGENT

You give serious and energetic effort to what you set out to do. Some people begin a project with good intentions but lack the ability to follow through and complete it. You are able to keep working on a project until it's done.

That's why you can be relied on to get a job done to the best of your ability. This strength will allow you to be successful in whatever you set out to do because you won't stop until you reach your objective.

*Related weaknesses: one-track mind, overindulgent self-interest, never slows down.*

### COURAGEOUS

You are able to hold to the course of action you believe you should take. You might become afraid in the face of danger, but you'll continue to do what you believe is the right thing to do because it's what you want to do.

Other people might start out, but they will fall by the wayside in the face of danger or difficulty. Not you. You have the strength of your convictions and the willingness to stand alone if necessary. As you keep your God-given courage balanced with sound thinking, you'll continue to be an inspiration for those people around you.

*Related weakness: recklessness.*

### DECISIVE

Unlike others who seem to waver back and forth because of doubt, you are able to make decisions. You have the ability to size up all the facts and make your choice based on what you believe is the best option available.

Being decisive doesn't mean you always make decisions quickly, nor does it mean that your decisions are easy. But when you make your decision, you move forward with it, and you don't feel a need for looking back and wondering. If the decision turns out to be wrong, you are able to accept it as a mistake and learn from it.

In the future, this trait can give the people you live and work with a great feeling of security and confidence in you. Just keep in mind that others may want to be included in making decisions, especially the ones that affect them.

*Related weaknesses: stubborn, overly independent.*

### GOAL-ORIENTED, PURPOSEFUL

Being purposeful is a strength of every achiever. It means you have the ability to give direction to your actions. You don't beat the air with aimless energy; you direct your actions toward accomplishments.

You have the strength of knowing what results you want to get, developing a course of action to reach those goals, and then reaching them. Other people may talk about things they want to do, but you allow your actions to speak for you. You get results!

You act on purpose, directing your energy and actions toward what you want to accomplish. Because you are a goal-oriented person, you can be relied on to use all of your resources to do what you commit yourself to do.

*Related weaknesses: inflexible, pushes too hard.*

### PERSEVERING

You have the ability to withstand hardships and overcome obstacles. We all have a breaking point when the going gets too rough. However, the breaking point for some people is shortly after they start. Not so for you.

You seem to be able to keep going even when you get tired and even though you might feel like quitting at times. Somehow you have the capacity to reach within yourself, or, possibly through your dependence on God, to find strength to keep going.

*Related weaknesses: overly competitive, never slows down.*

### DIRECT, STRAIGHTFORWARD

Being direct and straightforward means that you are honest and up front with people as you relate to them. They never have to wonder what you are thinking—you'll tell them!

This can be a refreshing strength in a day when some people just say what they think the other person wants to hear, or purposely try to deceive others. People can rely on you meaning what you say. As long as you temper this strength with tact, you'll find that most people greatly appreciate your being up front with them.

*Related weaknesses: tactless, blunt, harsh, disrespectful, mean.*

### CONFIDENT

You know your abilities, and you have a good sense of what you can and can't do with them. Being a confident person, you believe you can make a valuable contribution to other people, and you know you can use your strengths to make a difference in your world of interests.

Your confidence enables you to be free to put your best effort into whatever you're doing without being afraid of how it's coming across to other people. It also allows you to make mistakes without being crushed afterward. A person like you, who has the freedom to make mistakes, also has the freedom to succeed. Keep in mind that your show of confidence, balanced with a genuine humility, is a real inspiration to other people.

*Related weaknesses: self-sufficient, cocky.*

### RESOURCEFUL

You are able to deal quickly and effectively with problems. Some people run from anything that looks like a potential difficulty, but not you. It's not that you want things to be hard; you just see problems in a different way.

The people who run from difficulties feel that problems have little or no redeeming value. As a resourceful person, you see problems in a more positive way—as opportunities to find solutions. Sometimes you use the resources you already have available to find a solution. Or you devise your own ways to handle a problem. The bottom line is that you can be a very good problem-solver, and in the world in which we live, that's a valuable strength to possess.

*Related weaknesses: overly independent, scheming.*

# PRAISEWORTHY QUALITIES OF THE HIGH "I" IN YOUR LIFE

### PEOPLE-PERSON

There's no question about it: you are a people-person! You like your friends, and you want them to like you. You really want others to accept you.

Some people are uncomfortable when they are put in the spotlight. Not you. When you are up in front of others, you come alive. You love to entertain, make people laugh, and have fun with others. For you, it's the more the merrier.

You also have an ability to put people at ease. When there's a conflict brewing, you work to build bridges between people to help them get along better.

As long as you keep this strength balanced with the ability to stand firm in what you believe when others try to get you to do things you know are not right, you will have the ability to lead others without giving in to them.

*Related weaknesses: overly dependent on what others think and say about them, easily give in to peer pressure, make promises that are not kept, overcommits.*

### GOOD COMMUNICATOR

Words come easily for you. You are very gifted at expressing your thoughts, opinions, and ideas. You have the capacity to express yourself through words in a clear manner, so other people can easily understand your thoughts and ideas.

Positive communication is one of the main building blocks for positive relationships. It's also a powerful asset for anyone interested in influencing the lives of other people. Your communication skills will help you pass on to others the ideas you think are worthwhile and, in so doing, you can help shape the way other people think.

*Related weaknesses: talks too much, interrupts when others are talking, smooth talker, poor listener.*

### ENCOURAGER

You are good at coming alongside people and lifting their spirits with your sincere words and helpful actions. We all lose perspective every now and then, and we tend to feel a little down. That's when we need someone like you. You have the ability to forget yourself and your problems and help others see that things really can work out.

Encouragement takes many different forms. Sometimes you use words to build up another person; on other occasions you take some action to help a person in a time of need. Or you might take the time to be with someone, just understanding and being there. However you do it, your encouragement is a breath of fresh air to many people.

*Related weakness: insincere compliments.*

### EXPRESSIVE, DRAMATIC

You have a gift for talking so that other people clearly understand what you're saying. Some people just use plain old nouns and verbs to get across a point. You use an artist's canvas. When you talk, people listen with their imagination.

Many times you gesture with your hands to make your point. Your face shines with intense emotion, and the tone of your voice goes up and down. All this helps get your message across by drawing people into what you are saying.

That's a tremendous strength to have in communicating the emotions of what you say along with the truth. People can understand descriptive mental pictures far better than simple words. Your expressiveness helps other people see life so much more fully.

*Related weakness: exaggerates.*

### HUMOROUS

You look on the lighter side of situations and find humor in them. A person like you, with a good sense of humor, is fun to be around—not necessarily because everyone wants a good laugh, but because someone with a sense of humor usually has a more positive attitude.

Humor helps other people relax and can be used to relieve tense moments. People like you help the rest of us loosen up a little and learn that God knew what He was doing when He gave us the gift of laughter.

*Related weaknesses: wisecracker, clowning around, does not take things seriously (uses humor to ignore problems).*

### IMAGINATIVE

You are gifted with an active and creative imagination. You can form an image of something in your mind and see it clearly when there's nothing tangible to see. Imaginative people like you have created great works of art, literature, and drama; they have invented the machines and have come up with the new ideas and projects which have improved our lives.

Imagination is the mother of invention. Ideas open new frontiers.

Your imagination allows you to see possibilities in the future, things that haven't yet been planned.

With your imagination, you can bring a tremendous amount of good to our world, for God has given you the ability to see what can be, not simply what is!

*Related weakness: day dreamer, loses touch with reality.*

### ENTHUSIASTIC

You put your total enthusiastic interest and effort into the pursuit of what you want. You pour your full self into your activities. Some people simply go through the motions of life, but not you. You live life with a passion. Life for you is seldom routine; it's an opportunity for you to express to others what you believe is important.

You enjoy a faster pace, and you like the freedom to choose what you want to do next. This feeds your enthusiasm and keeps a smile on your face.

With this strength, you can make a great impact for good on the lives of many people, helping them look and feel more positively about what they are doing.

*Related weaknesses: disorganization, lack of objectivity.*

### PERSUASIVE

This means you have the ability to come up with words that cause others to agree with your ideas or your course of action. Others, as a result of your words, will either form a new attitude or take action that they would not have taken if it weren't for you.

Great leaders are persuasive people, for they have to get other people of various backgrounds and attitudes toward life to walk together toward specific objectives. You have an important ingredient for leadership, and you will find great demand for your skill as long as you use it in a positive way.

*Related weaknesses: manipulative, overbearing.*

### OPTIMISTIC, POSITIVE

You seem to look for the best in people and situations. That's what I call optimism. An optimistic person looks for, and actually expects, the best possible outcome in most situations.

Many people have eyes only for the negatives, and they focus too much on the possible problems they'll face in different situations. You have a hopeful, expectant attitude, even when things do not look promising. In spite of the circumstances, you do not easily get discouraged. When optimism is linked with a careful study of the facts, it can inspire other people to start working for the best, instead of settling for mediocrity.

Sure, you have some negative thoughts once in awhile, just like anyone else. Not every tough situation will seem to have good in it. But, overall, you are an upbeat person who is willing to work at seeing difficulties in a positive way. Your positive approach is the foundation upon which new plans can be made. It also helps raise the spirits of other people.

*Related weaknesses: idealistic, unrealistic, lack of objectivity, overly emotional even when presented with the facts; ignores facts in order to emphasize feelings.*

### SPONTANEOUS, FLEXIBLE

You enjoy activity, and you're able to jump into something at a moment's notice. Some people like to plan out an activity beforehand; planning is good, but there are times when it's better to do things on the spur of the moment. You have a knack for doing this.

You can pick up and go right away, and you enjoy the adventure of trying something new and different. Usually you are not disturbed if things don't go your way; you just adjust, "go with the flow," and make the best of it. You don't want to get bogged down in a bunch of details. You like to act on your gut reactions and explore your hunches. This makes you an enjoyable person to be with.

*Related weaknesses: impulsive, lack of urgency, disorganized.*

# Praiseworthy Qualities of the High "S" in Your Life

### Accepting

You help other people feel good about themselves. They know they can relax and be authentic around you—they don't need to pretend to be somebody they are not when they're with you.

By allowing people to be themselves, you give them the freedom to make mistakes. When people have the freedom to fail, they also feel free to take risks—which gives them the opportunity to achieve great things.

So, by accepting people, you are building within them the foundation upon which they will find success and fulfillment.

*Related weaknesses: lacking conviction, being too lenient.*

### Content

Most people desire to be satisfied in what they do, but not everyone attains it. Some people set such high standards for themselves that they never feel much sense of satisfaction and fulfillment in what they accomplish.

Being content or easygoing means that you have the capacity, even when problems arise, to be more positive than some people might be, and you actually see some benefits in the problems. This gives other people a more relaxed feeling around you. You have the kind of outlook that enables you to smell the roses of life each day.

*Related weaknesses: lazy, unmotivated, lacking initiative.*

### Helpful

It's easy in our world to be so caught up in what we're doing that we don't notice when other people might need a helping hand. But you notice, and you're willing to help even if it means going out of your way to do it. You're willing to help, not for any personal reward, but simply because you know a person needs help. You want to do what's best for that person, even if he shows little gratitude.

Most people say that the person who impresses them most is the person who is eager to lend a helping hand.

The people in your life know you care about them, and you will work at helping discover ways to resolve their problems. Your concern is no doubt a great encouragement for the people in your life. We need more helpful people like you in this world.

*Related weaknesses: overly accommodating, rescuer.*

### COOPERATIVE

Being cooperative means you have the ability to work with other people in an agreeable way. You are neither threatened by the input of others, nor are you domineering in expressing your ideas, even though you have good ideas to contribute. You believe other people also have good ideas, and you are willing to make personal sacrifices to get the best results when you know how they want something done.

You're a team player, and you know that two people can usually accomplish more working together than separately. Your ability to cooperate, as long as you keep contributing your own ideas, will be a plus in helping to get the best results in your projects.

*Related weaknesses: wishy-washy, overly accommodating, lacks assertiveness, gives in too easily.*

### SOFT-HEARTED, COMPASSIONATE

You hurt when other people hurt, and you are happy when others are happy. You live your own life, but you are able to experience what others are experiencing and feel what they are going through. Other people feel comfortable when they're with you because we all like to be with people who work at understanding us.

You won't simply feel sorry for someone—you'll go out of your way to help a person feel better. You can be a great comfort to people who are going through times of tragedy and sorrow, sometimes by just being there for them.

*Related weaknesses: pushover, easily influenced, overly burdened by the problems of others—assuming ownership of those problems.*

### SUBMISSIVE, OBEDIENT

Both followers and leaders must have this strength. Being obedient means that you are committed to live according to the boundaries set by your authorities (i.e., your parents, teachers, bosses).

You may not agree with everything your authorities decide, but you do give your best effort in helping to carry out the tasks and responsibilities you are given. In a society that often glorifies individuality, regardless of how it affects other people, you set an example of how things work more smoothly in a proper authority structure.

*Related weaknesses: pushover, weak-willed, willing to compromise personal sense of responsibility.*

### Good Listener

You tend to listen more than talk. You pay careful attention to what other people say, and you think before you speak so that what you say complements what the other person has just said.

What a great strength to have in developing relationships with other people! Some people are so interested in talking that they don't pay attention to what the other person is saying. They just wait for their chance to talk back. As you keep your strength of listening balanced with responding to what the other person said, you help people feel appreciated.

*Related weakness: non-communicative.*

### Steady

You feel most comfortable with routines and familiar ways of doing things. You feel uneasy when things change too quickly; you prefer things to stay the same.

In a world that seems to change every day, it's not always possible to keep things the same. Balancing your steady temperament with some flexibility in the right situations will help you process change more effectively. Because you are a stable person, you can be an anchor when the waters of our lives gets stormy.

*Related weaknesses: resists change or new ideas, inflexible, stubborn.*

### Modest

Being modest means you don't push yourself into the limelight for things you have either said or done. In other words, you don't go out of your way to call attention to yourself.

You feel more at home talking about the accomplishments of other people than about your own. You want to be appreciated, but not in a public way. Modest people like you are very refreshing in a look-at-me world.

*Related weaknesses: resists compliments, shrugs off praise, discounts own abilities.*

### Reliable

You can be depended on to do what you say you'll do when you say you'll do it. You give your best effort, even when it's inconvenient for you to do so. People depend on you; they know you do your duties in a responsible manner and you follow through on what you say you'll do.

If some unforeseen circumstance makes it impossible for you to keep your commitment, you'll try to notify the proper people ahead of time.

You'll give the same great quality effort each time, even if what you do is routine and you have to do the same thing over and over again.

You are able to give unswerving allegiance to either a person or a cause, even at great personal sacrifice. In sports, you would be called a "die hard" fan. In terms of civics, you would be called a patriot. Your strength of devotion is an inspiration to those with whom you work. Your word is as good as action. That's one of the reasons people have confidence in you. You can be trusted!

*Related weaknesses: overly accommodating, is easily taken advantage of.*

# PRAISEWORTHY QUALITIES OF THE HIGH "C" IN YOUR LIFE

## ANALYTICAL

What a great strength it is to be able to see a person or situation and easily see both strengths and weaknesses. You can quickly perceive things in people and situations that others have a more difficult time noticing.

When properly balanced with the discernment of knowing when to point out a weakness to someone and when to keep silent, your strength of being analytical can be used to make good things even better. Every planning committee needs at least one analytical person who can quickly size up the positives and negatives in a situation. We also need analytical people like you who can look within us and help us see what strengths we have.

*Related weaknesses: overly critical, cynical, overly analytical.*

## CURIOUS

You have a questioning mind. You are not satisfied with seeing that something works; you want to know how and why it works.

You have the kind of questioning mind that blazes new trails, looking for different answers, rather than settling for what has been. Thanks to curious people like you, we have made great advances in science, medicine, and technology. Curiosity, balanced with sensitivity to the needs of others, is a great strength when you use it to find new ways to benefit other people.

*Related weakness: nosy, asks too many questions, "interrogates" others.*

## CAUTIOUS

You like to do things in *your* time and in *your* way, rather than jump into something new and different. You think things through, evaluating possible choices and probable consequences before taking action. Being careful prevents you from making many rash and unwise decisions.

This strength keeps you from being pressured by others to do something you don't want to do before you are ready to do it. This can save you a lot of heartache in the future.

*Related weaknesses: unsociable, lack of boldness, skeptical, distrustful.*

**CONSCIENTIOUS**

You work hard and strive for excellence in all you do. You give focused attention to key details and enjoy performing tasks precisely and accurately. You make sure things are done right, and you are willing to stay on a job until all the loose ends are tied together.

Because of this strength, you are a valuable asset to any planning team. You insist that plans are completed before action is taken. Some people might get a little impatient with you because they want to get things going, but they will eventually see the wisdom in your approach.

*Related weaknesses: worries too much, perfectionistic.*

**OBJECTIVE**

You have the ability to look at all perspectives on a problem or decision. You are able to discern the facts and sort out feelings and opinions. You are even able to understand the feelings, views, and backgrounds of those who disagree with you.

This strength allows you to carefully weigh all relevant aspects of a problem without distorting them. This is an invaluable asset in any group.

*Related weaknesses: insensitive, unfeeling, lack of emotional response.*

**DISCERNING**

You have a good understanding of both people and situations. In a world that places so much emphasis on surface appearances and quick impressions, we need more people like you who won't be taken in just because something looks good or someone sounds reasonable.

You have the ability to grasp the reality that lies beneath the surface. In many situations, your intuition enables you not only to understand the truth, but also to know the right thing to do. The cutting edge of discernment reaches it's greatest potential when it is sharpened by principles from the Bible. As you can see, with this strength you are able to contribute greatly in working with people. So continue to think deeply about things to get a better grasp of what action you should take with the people you meet and the situations you face.

This strength can be used to help people who aren't getting along to come to a better understanding of each other. You're a valuable person to have in group situations!

*Related weaknesses: can be hard to follow this person's logic or pathway to conclusions.*

### SERIOUS MINDED, PREPARED

You take your responsibilities and your work seriously, and you desire to give your very best effort to what you choose to do. Because excellent results seldom happen by accident, you know that a best effort also requires good preparation. You have the ability to think ahead and plan what a task requires in terms of time, talent, and effort. This enables people to have confidence in what you do because they know you have put a great deal of thought into your actions.

*Related weaknesses: perfectionistic, takes too much time to complete assignments.*

### SELF-CONTROLLED

Having self-control means you're able to keep your emotions and actions in check and keep a cool head when other people might feel like exploding. You have a good grip on your desires, and you can say no to those actions that might be harmful to you.

Self-control also allows you to channel your energies in the direction you want to go. All successful people exercise this quality to accomplish what they set out to do.

*Related weakness: emotionless.*

### INDUSTRIOUS

Being industrious means you work hard at what you do. It seems that some people work harder trying to get out of work than they actually work, but not you. You aren't looking for an easy way out. You know that hard work will eventually pay off. That's why you can be relied on to get a job done to the best of your ability.

Your strength of being industrious allows you to be successful in whatever you set out to do because you won't stop until you get it just right. That also makes you a valuable asset for any project that needs a person with stick-to-it-iveness.

*Related weakness: too demanding or exacting, both of themselves and others (this may be hidden or below the surface, rather than spoken).*

### DOES THINGS CORRECTLY

You have high standards and you stick to them. You will not settle for doing less than your best, and you do not like any mistakes. Having things "right' is important to you. As long as you balance this strength with tolerance and you allow yourself and others to occasionally fail, you will contribute much to plans and the people in your life. This strength sets a good example for others.

*Related weaknesses: rigid, judgmental, "nit-picky."*

# SUMMARY OF THE DISC SYSTEM

| STYLE | D | I | S | C |
|---|---|---|---|---|
| **Basic Tendencies** | Fast-Paced<br>Task-oriented | Fast-Paced<br>People-oriented | Slower-Paced<br>People-Oriented | Slower-Paced<br>Task-oriented |
| **Greatest Strengths** | Decisive Action<br>Takes Charge<br>Gets Results<br>Self-Confident<br>Independent<br>Risk-Taker | Fun-Loving<br>Involved with Others<br>Enthusiastic<br>Emotional<br>Optimistic<br>Good Communicator | Patient<br>Easygoing<br>Team Player<br>Calming Influence<br>Steady, Stable<br>Good Follow-Through | Accurate<br>Analytical<br>Attentive to Key Details<br>High Standards<br>Intuitive<br>Controlled |
| **Natural Limitations** | Impatient<br>Stubborn<br>Harsh or Blunt | Disorganized<br>Not Detail-Oriented<br>Unrealistic | Indecisive<br>Over Accommodating<br>Too Passive<br>Sensitive | Too Critical<br>Perfectionistic<br>Overly Sarcastic |
| **Communication** | One Way<br>Direct<br>"Bottom Line" | Positive<br>Inspiring<br>Persuasive | Two Way<br>Best Listener<br>Empathetic<br>Feedback | Diplomatic<br>Keen Observer<br>Provides Details |
| **Fears** | Being Taken Advantage of | Loss of Social Approval | Loss of Stability | Irrational Acts, Criticism of Their Work |
| **Love Language** | Admiration | Acceptance and Approval | Appreciation | Affirmation |
| **Under Pressure** | Autocratic<br>Aggressive<br>Demanding | Emotional Attack<br>(But May Avoid Public Confrontation) | Acquiesces<br>Tolerates<br>Complies | Avoids, Withdraws,<br>Plans Strategy to Get Even |
| **Money Viewed As A Means Of** | Power | Freedom | Showing Love | Insuring Security |
| **Decision Making** | Quick:<br>Result-Focused<br>Very Few Facts | Impulsive<br>Whether It "Feels" Right | Relational:<br>Trusts in Others | Reluctant<br>Needs a Lot of Information |
| **Greatest Needs** | Challenges<br>Change<br>Choices<br>Direct Answers | Fun Activities<br>Social Recognition<br>Freedom from Details | Status Quo/Stability<br>Time to Adjust to Changes, Sincere Appreciation | Time to Do Quality Work<br>Facts<br>Time to Analyze |
| **Recharge** | Physical Activity | Social Time | "Nothing" Time | Private Time |

* Adapted from The Family Discovery Profile Manual, by Charles F. Boyd. Published by the Carlson Learning Company, © 1991. Used by Permission

APPENDIX C

# RECOMMENDED RESOURCES

## MUST-READ BOOKS ON PARENTING AND/OR UNDERSTANDING PEOPLE

Campbell, Ross. *How to Really Love Your Child.* Wheaton, Ill.: Victor Books, 1977, 1992.

Cline, Foster and Jim Fay. *Parenting with Love and Logic.* Colorado Springs, Co.: NavPress, 1990.

Kimmel, Tim. *Home-Grown Heroes.* Portland, Ore.: Multnomah Press, 1992.

Kimmel, Tim. *Raising Kids Who Turn Out Right.* Sisters, Ore.: Multnomah Books, 1993.

Narramore, Bruce. *Your Child's Hidden Needs.* Old Tappan, N.J.: Fleming H. Revell, 1990.

Rohm, Robert. *Positive Personality Profiles.* Atlanta: Personality Insights, Inc., 1993. (This book is based on the DISC system.)

Sloat, Donald. *The Dangers of Growing Up in a Christian Home.* Nashville: Thomas Nelson, 1986.

Smalley, Gary and John Trent. *The Blessing.* New York: Pocket Books, 1986.

Smalley, Gary and John Trent. *The Gift of Honor.* Nashville: Thomas Nelson, 1987.

Smalley, Gary. *The Key to Your Child's Heart.* Dallas: Word Publishing, 1992.

Smalley, Gary and John Trent. *The Treasure Tree.* Dallas: Word Publishing, 1990.

Smalley, Gary and John Trent. *The Two Sides of Love.* Pomona, Calif.: Focus on the Family, 1990.

Voges, Ken and Ron Braund. *Understanding How Others Misunderstand You.* Chicago: Moody Press, 1990. (This book is based on the DISC system.)

## RESOURCES FROM THE CARLSON LEARNING COMPANY
## (formerly Performax Systems, International)

The following are scientifically developed profiles that will help you understand yourself and others in terms of the DISC system. All profiles are self-scoring and self-interpreting.

*The Child Discovery Profile*

*The Teen Discovery Profile*

*The Child's Library of Classical Patterns*

*The Couple's Profile,* by Charles F. Boyd

*The Relationship Discovery Profile,* by Charles F. Boyd

*The Biblical Personal Profile System,* by Ken Voges

*The Couple's Profile Manual,* by Charles F. Boyd

*The Family Discovery Profile Manual,* by Charles F. Boyd

To order any of the above materials, contact your local Carlson Learning Network associate, or write the Carlson Learning Company, Carlson Parkway, P.O. Box 59159, Minneapolis, MN 55459-8247 (or call: 612-449-2856).

If you desire more information, write:
Charles and Karen Boyd
InSight Services
#21 Toulouse Court
Little Rock, Arkansas 72211